D0926562   75

LATIN'S NOT SO TOUGH!

LEVEL THREE ANSWER KEY

A Classical Latin Worktext
by
Karen Mohs

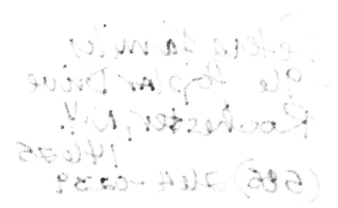

Dear Parent/Teacher:

This answer key is designed to assist you in teaching Latin Workbook Level Three.

Daily flashcard practice is essential. Please do not neglect this effective learning tool. The words for flashcard use are located at the end of the workbook.

Most importantly, continue to make this an enjoyable learning experience and a happy memory for both you and your student.

References for this series include *First Year Latin* by Charles Jenney, Jr., *Second Year Latin* by Charles Jenney, Jr., and *The New College Latin & English Dictionary* by John C. Traupman, Ph.D.

ISBN-13: 978-1-931842-61-7
ISBN-10: 1-931842-61-2

Greek 'n' Stuff
P.O. Box 882
Moline, IL 61266-0882
www.greeknstuff.com

Revised 2/06

SCHEDULE OF LESSONS
(PROPOSAL FOR LEVEL THREE)

In overview, the *Latin's Not So Tough!* workbooks are designed such that the student ideally completes one page per day (and practices his or her flashcards each day as well). (It should be noted that older students often complete more than one page per day when they are working in the early levels.) The workbooks were not designed within a framework of "lessons." Many parents have told us they appreciate this approach. It is easy to follow, without need of additional parent/teacher preparation and scheduling.

However, some parents/teachers prefer the "lesson" approach. Please be aware that this "Schedule of Lessons" is an artificial grid placed over a series not written with this grid in mind. The assigned pages are arbitrary and should be modified so the student can progress through the workbooks at a pace suitable to his or her age/skill level.

A note about our methodology:
Referred to by some as the "Saxon of Latin," this series begins gently and advances gradually, providing plenty of reinforcement through a wide variety of workbook activities and translation exercises. By introducing new concepts slowly, *Latin's Not So Tough!* avoids the pitfall common to many foreign language courses whereby the student suddenly faces a steep learning curve, becomes frustrated, fails to internalize the language, and develops an aversion to foreign language study in general. The overwhelming response from those using *Latin's Not So Tough!* can be summed up by the words we hear so often: "This is my student's favorite subject."

Lesson 1
Pages 1-6 - Alphabet review

Teacher tip:
Latin's Not So Tough! teaches classical pronunciation. Because the distinctions between classical and ecclesiastical pronunciations are relatively minor, students generally do not find it difficult to switch from one pronunciation to another. For a comparison of the classical and ecclesiastical pronunciations, see pages 4-6 of *The New College Latin & English Dictionary* by John C. Traupman, Ph.D. For a thorough examination of pronunciation, see pages 1-8 of *New Latin Grammar* by Charles E. Bennett or pages 1-6 of *Latin Grammar* by B.L. Gildersleeve & G. Lodge.

Lesson 2
Pages 7-10 - Diphthong and Special Consonant review

Lesson 3
 Pages 11-15 - Vocabulary review - Part 1

Teacher tip:
  Use the derivatives to help your student learn the vocabulary. One parent using this series chooses a derivative and has her students write that derivative as a hint in the large box in which the Latin vocabulary word is first taught. For example, when she teaches "ager," she has her students write "agriculture" in the box. If the word does not have an English derivative, such as "pugnō," she thinks of a silly saying, such as "The **pug** dog likes to fight." Other parents point out derivatives encountered in daily activities and have their students attempt to recall the Latin vocabulary words from which the English words come. Many such techniques are helpful in reinforcing the vocabulary.

  As is generally true when translating from one language into another, a particular Latin word can often have a range of English meanings. To discern the correct choice, translators rely on context. However, your student is just beginning to learn Latin. At this point in his studies, he is encountering words in isolation. Later in this workbook, he will begin translating short sentences in isolation. Without context, he has no basis for knowing which words most closely render the original author's meaning. Any of the possible answers should be considered correct.

English derivatives:
  voco (vocabulary, vocation, avocation, advocate, convoke, revoke, invoke, evoke, provoke, vocable)
  puer (puerile, puerilely, puerileness, puerilism, puerility, puerperium)
  dō (date, datum, dative, edition, tradition, perdition, add, dado, dice)
  aqua (aqua, aquarium, aqueduct, aqueous, aquamarine, aquatic, semiaquatic, aquatint, aquacade, aquanaut, aquaplane, aquarelle, Aquarius, gouache, ewer)
  fēmina (female, feminine, effeminate, femininity, femme, feme)
  silva (silva, sylvan, savage, selva, silvichemical, silvicolous, silviculture, sylph, sylvatic)
  īnsula (isle, peninsula, isolate, isolation, insulate, insular)
  laudō (laud, laudable, laudatory, allow)
  vīta (vita, vital, vitality, vitamin, revitalize, devitalize, viable)
  porta (porter, portal, portico, porch, portcullis, porthole)
  memoria (memorial, memory, memoir, memorize, memorable, memorandum)
  nāvigō (navy, navigate, navigation, navigable)

Lesson 4

Pages 16-20 - Vocabulary review - Part 2

English derivatives:

fortūna (fortune, fortunate, fortunately, unfortunate)

via (via, viatic, viaduct, trivial, trivium, quadrivium, envoy, previous, pervious, impervious, obvious, devious, deviate, voyage, convey)

portō (portfolio, porter, portable, rapport, deport, disport, export, purport, comport, import, transport, support, report, portage, portamento, portative)

quid (quidnunc, quiddity, quip)

tuba (tuba, tubaist, tubist, saxtuba)

ager (agriculture, agrarian, peregrine, pilgrim, agronomy)

parō (parasol, rampart, emperor, disparate, pare, apparatus, prepare, repair, parade, separate, parapet, parachute, parador, parlay, parry, parament)

amīcus (amigo, amity, amicable, amiable, amiably, amiability)

spectō (spectator, spectacle, bespectacled, speculate, expect, aspect, respect, inspect, prospect, suspect, circumspect)

nātūra (nature, natural, supernatural, preternatural)

campus (campus, camp, campaign, champion, scamper, campo, campestral, campesino, champerty)

occupō (occupation, occupy)

nauta (nautical)

vīlla (villa, village, villain, villanelle)

littera (literal, literary, literate, illiterate, alliteration, transliterate, obliterate, letter, literatim)

Lesson 5

Pages 21-26 - Vocabulary review - Part 3

English derivatives:

ubi (ubiquity, ubiety, alibi)

filius (filial, filiate, affiliate)

patria (repatriate, expatriate, patriarch)

amō (amorous, amateur, amative, paramour, inamorato, amatory)

lingua (lingua, language, linguist, linguistics, bilingual, lingo, linguine, lingulate, languet)

equus (equine, equestrian, equitant, equisetum)

poēta (poet, poetry, poetical, poetaster)

annus (annual, annals, anniversary, millenium, annuity, superannuated, perennial, biennium, triennium)

pugnō (pugnacious, repugn, inexpugnable, oppugn, impugn)

terra (terra, terra cotta, terrier, terrarium, territory, terrace, inter, tureen, mediterranean, subterranean, terrestrial, terrene, terreplein, parterre, terraqueous, terrigenous, terricolous)

gladius (gladiator, gladiate, gladiolus, glaive)

| prōvincia (province, provincial, provincialize) |

Lesson 6

Pages 27-30 - Accusative case - singular (first and second declensions)

~~~~~~

The Big Picture - You Are Here

Declensions (Nouns)					
first declension	**second declension**	third declension	third i-stem declension	fourth declension	fifth declension
feminine **masculine**	**masculine** -us **masculine** -ius masculine -er neuter	masculine/ feminine neuter	masculine/ feminine neuter	masculine/ feminine neuter	masculine/ feminine

SINGULAR

-a	nominative	-us	nom.	nom.	nom.	nom.	nom.
-ae	genitive	-ī	gen.	gen.	gen.	gen.	gen.
-ae	dative	-ō	dat.	dat.	dat.	dat.	dat.
-am	**accusative**	**-um**	**acc.**	acc.	acc.	acc.	acc.
-ā	ablative	-ō	abl.	abl.	abl.	abl.	abl.

PLURAL

-ae	nominative	-ī	nom.	nom.	nom.	nom.	nom.
-ārum	genitive	-ōrum	gen.	gen.	gen.	gen.	gen.
-īs	dative	-īs	dat.	dat.	dat.	dat.	dat.
-ās	accusative	-ōs	acc.	acc.	acc.	acc.	acc.
-īs	ablative	-īs	abl.	abl.	abl.	abl.	abl.

For more information on the first and second declensions, number, gender, and case, see pages 12-18 of Bennett's *New Latin Grammar* or pages 13-17 of Gildersleeve's *Latin Grammar*. For more information on word order, see pages 227-231 of Bennett's *New Latin Grammar*.

~~~~~~

~~~~~~

Teacher tip:
    Origin of case names:
        Nominative: from nōmināre - to name
        Genitive: from genitus, past participle of gignere - to beget
        Dative: from datus, past participle of dare - to give
        Accusative: from accūsātus, past participle of accūsāre - to accuse
        Ablative: from ablātus - carried away
    For common case uses, see the appendix.

    When your student is ready to begin a good supplementary Latin reader, we recommend *Familia Romana*, which is Part One of *Lingua Latina Per Se Illustrata* by Hans H. Orberg. Allow your student to progress at his or her own pace through this reader.

~~~~~~

Lesson 6 (continued)

~~~~~~

Translation walk-through (pages 27 and 28):

On page 27, the Latin *accusative* case is introduced. This case is used as the *direct object* [*receiver* of the action] in English grammar. An example of the English word "ball" *receiving* the action would be: "I hit the ball." That is, "the ball" is being hit. It is thus *receiving* the action. (Your student need not be concerned about English or Latin grammatical terms at this time.)

Two examples are given in the first box on page 27 as follows:

Amō puellam. - As your student learned in Level 2, "amō" means "I like." He should recognize that "puellam" is a variation of the vocabulary word "puella," which means "the girl." ("Puella" is the form used when "the girl" is the one *performing* the action. This is called the *subject* of the sentence in English grammar.)

Amō fīlium. - Again, as your student learned in Level 2, "amō" means "I like." He should recognize that "fīlium" is a variation of the vocabulary word "fīlius," which means "the son." ("Fīlius" is the form used when "the son" is the one *performing* the action, the *subject* of the sentence in English grammar.)

In both of these examples, the second word of the sentence ("puellam" or "fīlium") *receives* the action of the verb "amō." They both play the same role in their sentences. That is, they are both functioning as our English *direct object*. However, an important difference exists between them. The original words ("puella" and "fīlius") started out with different endings (-a and -us).

In the second box on page 27, your student will notice certain "clues." The first clue states that the -us ending on words like "fīlius," "equus," and "amīcus" changes from -us to -um. The second clue states that the -a ending on words like "puella," "nauta," and "vīlla" changes from -a to -am. That is all your student needs to know at this point. (Later, he will learn that these two words belong to the first two of five categories of Latin nouns called *declensions*. A declension is simply a regular way in which the endings of nouns change so that they can play the roles of different parts of the sentence such as *subject*, *direct object*, *indirect object*, etc.)

In summary, at this point in the workbook, if the original vocabulary word ends in -us, your student simply changes that -us to -um to make the word *receive* the action of the verb. (In the case of "Amō fīlium," the son *receives* the action because it is the son whom I like.) If the original vocabulary word ends in -a, simply change that -a to -am to make the word *receive* the action of the verb. (In the case of "Amō puellam," it is the girl whom I like.)

The exercises on page 28 apply this concept. We will study one example.

Lesson 6 (continued)

The first sentence begins with the word "vocō." Your student knows that this word means "I call." (Please note the "I" in "I call." Later, your student will learn to change the ending on verbs like "vocō" to mean "you call" or "we call" or "he calls" or "the _____ calls," etc.) Two choices are given to complete this sentence: "puellam" and "puella." "Puella" will not work because, as explained above, the -a ending indicates that "the girl" is the one *performing* the action. However, in this sentence, "the girl" cannot be the one *performing* the action because the verb "vocō" means "**I** call." Hence, "I" must be the one *performing* the action (the *subject* of the sentence). That leaves the second choice, "puellam," which is acceptable because "the girl" can be the "*receiver* of the action." In other words, it is "the girl" whom I call. The sentence is translated, "I call the girl."

Your student should think through the steps given in this example as he works on the exercises that follow.

~~~~~~

~~~~~~

Teacher tip:

Regarding word order, the important thing to remember is that there usually is not one correct way of ordering the Latin words in a sentence. The Latin sentence for "I call the girl" could easily be translated either "Vocō puellam" or "Puellam vocō." As mentioned in the note at the bottom of page 28, the most usual order would be "Puellam vocō" because of the tendency to place the verb last. "Vocō puellam" would be used if the fact that "I call" is emphasized. (Varying word order in this exercise is used to acquaint the student with the different possibilities for Latin word order.) Please do not mark as incorrect a sentence with a word order differing from that in the answer key. With every sentence, there are usually multiple possibilities for the order of the words.

~~~~~~

Lesson 7
Pages 31-34 - Accusative case - plural (first and second declensions)

~~~~~~

The Big Picture - You Are Here

Declensions (Nouns)						
first declension	**second declension**	third declension	third i-stem declension	fourth declension	fifth declension	
feminine **masculine**	**masculine -us** **masculine -ius** masculine -er neuter	masculine/ feminine neuter	masculine/ feminine neuter	masculine/ feminine neuter	masculine/ feminine	
SINGULAR	-a nominative	-us nom.	nom.	nom.	nom.	nom.
	-ae genitive	-ī gen.	gen.	gen.	gen.	gen.
	-ae dative	-ō dat.	dat.	dat.	dat.	dat.
	-am accusative	-um acc.	acc.	acc.	acc.	acc.
	-ā ablative	-ō abl.	abl.	abl.	abl.	abl.
PLURAL	-ae nominative	-ī nom.	nom.	nom.	nom.	nom.
	-ārum genitive	-ōrum gen.	gen.	gen.	gen.	gen.
	-īs dative	-īs dat.	dat.	dat.	dat.	dat.
	-ās accusative	**-ōs acc.**	acc.	acc.	acc.	acc.
	-īs ablative	-īs abl.	abl.	abl.	abl.	abl.

For more information on the first and second declensions, number, gender, and case, see pages 12-18 of Bennett's *New Latin Grammar* or pages 13-17 of Gildersleeve's *Latin Grammar.*

~~~~~~
~~~~~~

Translation hint (page 32, sentence 7):
Some students wonder why the form "litterās" (instead of "litteram") is used in sentence 7 on page 32. Have your student refer to page 20. There he will see that the Latin word "littera," when plural, means "the epistle." (Think of an epistle as many "letters of the alphabet" put together on one page.) Thus, on page 32, the correct form of "littera" would be the plural form ("litterās"), rather than the singular form ("litteram"), since a plural form is required for the meaning to be "the epistle."

~~~~~~

Lesson 8
Pages 35-38 - First person - singular and plural (first conjugation)

The Big Picture - You Are Here

Conjugations (Verbs)						
MOOD indicative / subjunctive / imperative	**TENSE** **present** perfect / imperfect pluperfect / future future perfect				**VOICE** **active** / passive	
first conjugation	second conjugation	third conjugation	third i-stem conjugation	fourth conjugation	irregular	
SINGULAR -ā+ō=ō **1st person**	1st	1st	1st	1st	1st	
-ā+s=ās 2nd person	2nd	2nd	2nd	2nd	2nd	
-ā+t=at 3rd person	3rd	3rd	3rd	3rd	3rd	
PLURAL -ā+mus=āmus **1st person**	1st	1st	1st	1st	1st	
-ā+tis=ātis 2nd person	2nd	2nd	2nd	2nd	2nd	
-ā+nt=ant 3rd person	3rd	3rd	3rd	3rd	3rd	

For more information on the first conjugation, see pages 58-61 of Bennett's *New Latin Grammar* or pages 72-75 of Gildersleeve's *Latin Grammar*.

Translation hint (page 36, right column, second row):

Some students wonder why the form "vītam" (instead of "vīta") is given as the correct translation of "life." (Actually, "vīta" would be the most obvious answer if it were given as a choice, but it is not.)

To understand why "vītam" is the correct choice of the four possible answers, your student should imagine the word "life" used in an English sentence. One use could be, "The life of the man was long." In this case, the Latin word would be "vīta." Another use could be, "The man saves the life of the boy." In this case, "life" is *receiving* the action of the verb "saves." (*What* does the man save? He saves the "life." Again, this is called a *direct object* in English grammar.)

As your student learned on page 27, when a singular word like "puella" *receives* the action of the verb, the ending -a should be changed to -am. The same applies to the Latin word "vīta." Hence, in the above example, "The man saves the life of the boy," the Latin word for "life" would be spelled "vītam."

In conclusion, since "vīta" was not given as a possibility, the only correct choice must be "vītam."

Lesson 9
Pages 39-42 - Genitive case - singular (first and second declensions)

~~~~~~

The Big Picture - You Are Here

<table>
<tr><td colspan="12" align="center">Declensions
(Nouns)</td></tr>
<tr>
<td colspan="2" align="center"><b>first
declension</b></td>
<td colspan="2" align="center"><b>second
declension</b></td>
<td align="center">third
declension</td>
<td align="center">third i-stem
declension</td>
<td align="center">fourth
declension</td>
<td align="center">fifth
declension</td>
</tr>
<tr>
<td colspan="2"><b>feminine</b>

<b>masculine</b></td>
<td colspan="2"><b>masculine</b> -us

<b>masculine</b> -ius

masculine -er

neuter</td>
<td>masculine/
feminine

neuter</td>
<td>masculine/
feminine

neuter</td>
<td>masculine/
feminine

neuter</td>
<td>masculine/
feminine</td>
</tr>
<tr>
<td rowspan="5">SINGULAR</td>
<td>-a　　nominative</td>
<td colspan="2">-us　　nom.</td>
<td>nom.</td>
<td>nom.</td>
<td>nom.</td>
<td>nom.</td>
</tr>
<tr>
<td><b>-ae　　genitive</b></td>
<td colspan="2"><b>-ī　　gen.</b></td>
<td>gen.</td>
<td>gen.</td>
<td>gen.</td>
<td>gen.</td>
</tr>
<tr>
<td>-ae　　dative</td>
<td colspan="2">-ō　　dat.</td>
<td>dat.</td>
<td>dat.</td>
<td>dat.</td>
<td>dat.</td>
</tr>
<tr>
<td>-am　　accusative</td>
<td colspan="2">-um　　acc.</td>
<td>acc.</td>
<td>acc.</td>
<td>acc.</td>
<td>acc.</td>
</tr>
<tr>
<td>-ā　　ablative</td>
<td colspan="2">-ō　　abl.</td>
<td>abl.</td>
<td>abl.</td>
<td>abl.</td>
<td>abl.</td>
</tr>
<tr>
<td rowspan="5">PLURAL</td>
<td>-ae　　nominative</td>
<td colspan="2">-ī　　nom.</td>
<td>nom.</td>
<td>nom.</td>
<td>nom.</td>
<td>nom.</td>
</tr>
<tr>
<td>-ārum　　genitive</td>
<td colspan="2">-ōrum　　gen.</td>
<td>gen.</td>
<td>gen.</td>
<td>gen.</td>
<td>gen.</td>
</tr>
<tr>
<td>-īs　　dative</td>
<td colspan="2">-īs　　dat.</td>
<td>dat.</td>
<td>dat.</td>
<td>dat.</td>
<td>dat.</td>
</tr>
<tr>
<td>-ās　　accusative</td>
<td colspan="2">-ōs　　acc.</td>
<td>acc.</td>
<td>acc.</td>
<td>acc.</td>
<td>acc.</td>
</tr>
<tr>
<td>-īs　　ablative</td>
<td colspan="2">-īs　　abl.</td>
<td>abl.</td>
<td>abl.</td>
<td>abl.</td>
<td>abl.</td>
</tr>
</table>

For more information on the first and second declensions, number, gender, and case, see pages 12-18 of Bennett's *New Latin Grammar* or pages 13-17 of Gildersleeve's *Latin Grammar.*

~~~~~~

~~~~~~

Teacher tip:

The *possessive* use of the *genitive* case can be translated into English either with an apostrophe and the letter *s* ('s) or with the words "of the."

When encountering a Latin sentence containing several nouns along with a genitive that shows possession, your student may be uncertain as to which of the nouns the genitive modifies. As a general principle, he should assume that the genitive modifies the nearest noun.

At times, however, the genitive is placed between two nouns and thus is equally close to either one. In such cases, the tendency in Latin to place the possessive genitive directly after the noun it modifies should influence your student's translation. For example, the sentence "Fīlia amīcī equum amat" could possibly mean "The daughter loves the horse of the friend," but it most likely means "The daughter of the friend loves the horse" since the genitive amīcī is probably following the word it modifies, which in this case is fīlia. (It is important to remember that this is merely a tendency. Your student will learn other word order tendencies as he progresses in his Latin studies.)

Only by knowing the "greater context" beyond the isolated sentence can one determine with certainty the author's intended meaning. In the case of

Lesson 9 (continued)

isolated sentences (such as those in this series), any grammatically correct answers should be accepted.

~~~~~~

~~~~~~

Translation tip (page 40, lower section, sentence 2):
    The Latin word "littera" (which means "a letter of the alphabet" when singular) has a curious meaning in the plural. If your student thinks of an epistle or a letter (of correspondence) being made up of many letters of the alphabet, he will have a glimpse into the plural meaning of "littera." (See the definition of "littera" on page 20.)

~~~~~~

****
QUIZ #1 (optional)
****

Lesson 10
Pages 43-50 - New vocabulary - Part 1, vocabulary practice

> *English derivatives:*
> lēgātus (legacy, legate)
> lūdus (ludicrous, interlude, elude, elusive, allude, allusion, illusion, delude, prelude, postlude, prolusion, collude, collusion, ludic, legate, legacy)
> appellō (appeal, appellate, appellative, appellation, appellant)
> servus (serve, servant, service, servile, sergeant, servitude, serf, concierge, sirvente, servomotor)
> nūntius and nūntiō (announce, pronounce, denounce, renounce, enunciate, nuncio, internuncio)
> nārrō (narrate, narrator, narration, narrative, narratability, narratable)
> fāma (fame, famous, famously, famousness, infamy, infamous, infamously, infamousness, defame)
> populus (popular, popularity, popularly, popularize, populate, population, depopulate, populace, populous, people, public, poplar, pueblo)
> rēgīna (Regina)
> exspectō (expect, expectation, expectant, expectance, expectancy, expectative, expectable, expectably, expectedly)

Lesson 11
Pages 51-56 - New vocabulary - Part 2, vocabulary practice

> *English derivatives:*
> habitō (inhabit, inhabitable, habitat, habitant, habitation, habitable, cohabit, cohabitation, binnacle)

Lesson 11 (continued)

> nunc (quidnunc)
> fābula (fable, fabulous, fabulist, fabulate, confabulate, confabulation)
> dēlectō (delectable, delectably, delectability, delectation, delight,
>   dilettante)
> labōrō (laboratory, labor, laborer, laborious, collaborate, collaboration,
>   elaborate, elaboration, belabor)
> causa (cause, causable, causeless, causerie, because, accuse, accuser,
>   recuse, excuse)
> socius (society, social, sociable, sociably, associate, association,
>   associative, dissociate, consociate)
> dīligentia (diligence)
> convocō (convoke, convocation, convocational)

Lesson 12

Pages 57-62 - Vocabulary and sentence practice - Part 1

Translation walk-through (page 59, three sentences):
Your student is asked to translate three sentences from English to Latin.
1. I praise the friendliness of the poet.

Your student first locates and translates the verb ("I praise"). The Latin word for "I praise" is "laudō."

Next, your student looks for a word that tells *who* or *what* I praise. He finds "the friendliness." (In English grammar, this is the *direct object*. In Latin grammar, this is the *accusative* case. It is the *receiver* of the action. That is, it tells *what* is being praised. Your student need not be concerned about the English or Latin grammatical terms at this time. He will begin learning terminology in Level 4.) The Latin word meaning "the friendliness" is "amīcitia." Because it tells *what* I praise and thus *receives* the action of the verb, the -a ending must be changed to -am. (See page 27.) The word becomes "amīcitiam."

For the final step, your student translates the words "of the poet." He knows that the Latin word for "the poet" is "poēta." As he learned on page 39, the -a ending must be changed to -ae to show that "the friendliness" belongs to the poet. (That is, friendliness is a characteristic of the poet.) (In English grammar, this is called *possession*. In Latin grammar, it is called the *genitive* case.) The word becomes "poētae."

Please recall that Latin word order can vary. The verb is often last, but it also stands in other positions based on the author's intended emphasis. Without context, emphasis is difficult or impossible to discern. Thus, when translating isolated sentences, any word order should be accepted.
2. We please the nations of the son.

Your student first locates and translates the verb ("we please"). He knows that the Latin word for "I please" is "dēlectō." As he learned on page 35, the -ō ending must be changed to -āmus to change the meaning from "**I** do something" to "**we** do something." The word becomes

Lesson 12 (continued)

"dēlectāmus."

   Next, your student looks for a word that tells *who* or *what* we please. He finds "the nations." The Latin word meaning "the nation" is "populus." Because it tells *what* we please and thus *receives* the action of the verb, the -us ending must be changed to -um. (See page 27.) However, the word in this sentence is plural ("the nation*s*"). As your student learned on page 31, the -um ending must be changed to -ōs to mean "more than one." The word becomes "populōs."

   For the final step, your student translates the words "of the son." He knows that the Latin word for "the son" is "fīlius." As he learned on page 39, the -ius ending must be changed to -ī to show that "the nations" belong to the son. The word becomes "fīlī."

3. I tell the wife's stories.

   Your student first locates and translates the verb ("I tell"). The Latin word for "I tell" is "nārrō."

   Next, your student looks for a word that tells *who* or *what* I tell. He finds "the stories." The Latin word meaning "the story" is "fābula." Because it tells *what* I tell and thus *receives* the action of the verb, the -a ending must be changed to -am. (See page 27.) However, the word in this sentence is plural ("the stor*ies*"). As your student learned on page 31, the -am ending must be changed to -ās to mean "more than one." The word becomes "fābulās."

   For the final step, your student translates the words "the wife's" (which means the same as "of the wife"). He knows that the Latin word for "the wife" is "fēmina." As he learned on page 39, the -a ending must be changed to -ae to show that "the stories" belong to the wife. The word becomes "fēminae."

Lesson 13
   Pages 63-66 - Vocabulary and sentence practice - Part 2

Latin Workbook - Level 3
Copyright © 1998 by Karen Mohs

Lesson 14
Pages 67-70 - Genitive case - plural (first and second declensions)

The Big Picture - You Are Here

Declensions (Nouns)						
	first declension	**second declension**	third declension	third i-stem declension	fourth declension	fifth declension
	feminine **masculine**	**masculine -us** **masculine -ius** masculine -er neuter	masculine/ feminine neuter	masculine/ feminine neuter	masculine/ feminine neuter	masculine/ feminine
SINGULAR	-a nominative	-us nom.	nom.	nom.	nom.	nom.
	-ae genitive	-ī gen.	gen.	gen.	gen.	gen.
	-ae dative	-ō dat.	dat.	dat.	dat.	dat.
	-am accusative	-um acc.	acc.	acc.	acc.	acc.
	-ā ablative	-ō abl.	abl.	abl.	abl.	abl.
PLURAL	-ae nominative	-ī nom.	nom.	nom.	nom.	nom.
	-ārum genitive	**-ōrum gen.**	gen.	gen.	gen.	gen.
	-īs dative	-īs dat.	dat.	dat.	dat.	dat.
	-ās accusative	-ōs acc.	acc.	acc.	acc.	acc.
	-īs ablative	-īs abl.	abl.	abl.	abl.	abl.

For more information on the first and second declensions, number, gender, and case, see pages 12-18 of Bennett's *New Latin Grammar* or pages 13-17 of Gildersleeve's *Latin Grammar*.

Lesson 15
Pages 71-74 - Third person - singular (first conjugation)

The Big Picture - You Are Here

Conjugations (Verbs)						
MOOD **indicative** subjunctive imperative	**TENSE** **present** perfect imperfect pluperfect future future perfect		**VOICE** **active** passive			
	first conjugation	second conjugation	third conjugation	third i-stem conjugation	fourth conjugation	irregular
SINGULAR	-ā+ō=ō 1st person	1st	1st	1st	1st	1st
	-ā+s=ās 2nd person	2nd	2nd	2nd	2nd	2nd
	-ā+t=at **3rd person**	3rd	3rd	3rd	3rd	3rd
PLURAL	-ā+mus=āmus 1st person	1st	1st	1st	1st	1st
	-ā+tis=ātis 2nd person	2nd	2nd	2nd	2nd	2nd
	-ā+nt=ant 3rd person	3rd	3rd	3rd	3rd	3rd

Lesson 15 (continued)

For more information on the first conjugation, see pages 58-61 of Bennett's *New Latin Grammar* or pages 72-75 of Gildersleeve's *Latin Grammar*.

~~~~~~

Lesson 16

Pages 75-78 - Nominative case - singular (first and second declensions)

~~~~~~

The Big Picture - You Are Here

Declensions (Nouns)							
	first declension		**second declension**	third declension	third i-stem declension	fourth declension	fifth declension
	feminine masculine		masculine -us masculine -ius masculine -er neuter	masculine/ feminine neuter	masculine/ feminine neuter	masculine/ feminine neuter	masculine/ feminine
SINGULAR	-a	**nominative**	-us	**nom.**	nom.	nom.	nom.	nom.
	-ae	genitive	-ī	gen.	gen.	gen.	gen.	gen.
	-ae	dative	-ō	dat.	dat.	dat.	dat.	dat.
	-am	accusative	-um	acc.	acc.	acc.	acc.	acc.
	-ā	ablative	-ō	abl.	abl.	abl.	abl.	abl.
PLURAL	-ae	nominative	-ī	nom.	nom.	nom.	nom.	nom.
	-ārum	genitive	-ōrum	gen.	gen.	gen.	gen.	gen.
	-īs	dative	-īs	dat.	dat.	dat.	dat.	dat.
	-ās	accusative	-ōs	acc.	acc.	acc.	acc.	acc.
	-īs	ablative	-īs	abl.	abl.	abl.	abl.	abl.

For more information on the first and second declensions, number, gender, and case, see pages 12-18 of Bennett's *New Latin Grammar* or pages 13-17 of Gildersleeve's *Latin Grammar*.

~~~~~~

~~~~~~

Translation walk-through (page 77, sentence 3):

Your student is asked to translate this sentence from Latin to English. In Latin, one must carefully notice the ending on each word. The endings are by far more important in determining the role a word plays in a sentence than the placement of the word (although placement can at times be important as well). (In simple English sentences, the first word is often the subject. In Latin, the ending tells us which word is the subject, regardless of where that word is placed in the sentence.)

Your student first locates and translates the verb ("parat"). He should recognize this word as a form of "parō" which means "I prepare" or "I prepare for." As he learned on page 71, the -ō ending changes to -at to indicate that he (she or it) does something. Thus, the meaning of "parat" is "he (she or it) prepares."

Lesson 16 (continued)

Now your student must look for a word that tells *who* or *what* "he, she, or it" is? (In English grammar, this is the *subject* of the sentence. In Latin grammar, this is the *nominative* case. It is the *doer* of the action. That is, it tells *who* or *what* is doing the preparing. Again, your student need not be concerned about the English or Latin grammatical terms at this time. He will begin learning terminology in Level 4.) This Latin word is easy to find because it is the vocabulary form of the word. (See page 75.) The word is "fēmina," which means "the woman" or "the wife." So far, sentence 3 reads, "The woman (or the wife) prepares."

Next, your student looks for a word that tells *who* or *what* the woman (or the wife) prepares. To be the *receiver* of the action, the Latin word must end with -am or -um (or, if plural, with -ās or -ōs). He finds "equōs," which means "the horses." So far, sentence 3 reads, "The woman (or the wife) prepares the horses."

For the final step, your student must translate the words "nautae" and "lēgātī." As he learned on page 39, the endings on both these words (-ae and -ī) are used to show *possession*. "Nautae" ("of the sailor") stands nearest to "fēmina." Thus, the most likely translation is "the wife of the sailor" or "the sailor's wife." "Lēgātī" ("of the lieutenant") stands nearest to "equōs." Thus, the most likely translation is "the horses of the lieutenant" or "the lieutenant's horses." The final translation of sentence 3 reads, "The sailor's wife prepares the lieutenant's horses."

Please note that your student will learn other uses of the -ae and the -ī endings as he progresses through this workbook.

~~~~~~

Lesson 17
Pages 79-82 - Third person - plural (first conjugation)

~~~~~~

The Big Picture - You Are Here

Conjugations (Verbs)					
MOOD **indicative** subjunctive imperative	**TENSE** **present** imperfect future	perfect pluperfect future perfect		**VOICE** **active** passive	
first conjugation	second conjugation	third conjugation	third i-stem conjugation	fourth conjugation	irregular
SINGULAR -ā+ō=ō 1st person	1st	1st	1st	1st	1st
-ā+s=ās 2nd person	2nd	2nd	2nd	2nd	2nd
-ā+t=at 3rd person	3rd	3rd	3rd	3rd	3rd
PLURAL -ā+mus=āmus 1st person	1st	1st	1st	1st	1st
-ā+tis=ātis 2nd person	2nd	2nd	2nd	2nd	2nd
-ā+nt=ant **3rd person**	3rd	3rd	3rd	3rd	3rd

Lesson 17 (continued)

For more information on the first conjugation, see pages 58-61 of Bennett's *New Latin Grammar* or pages 72-75 of Gildersleeve's *Latin Grammar*.

~~~~~~

Lesson 18

Pages 83-86 - Nominative case - plural (first and second declensions)

~~~~~~

The Big Picture - You Are Here

	Declensions (Nouns)					
	first declension	**second declension**	third declension	third i-stem declension	fourth declension	fifth declension
	feminine **masculine**	**masculine** -us **masculine** -ius masculine -er neuter	masculine/ feminine neuter	masculine/ feminine neuter	masculine/ feminine neuter	masculine/ feminine
SINGULAR	-a nominative	-us nom.	nom.	nom.	nom.	nom.
	-ae genitive	-ī gen.	gen.	gen.	gen.	gen.
	-ae dative	-ō dat.	dat.	dat.	dat.	dat.
	-am accusative	-um acc.	acc.	acc.	acc.	acc.
	-ā ablative	-ō abl.	abl.	abl.	abl.	abl.
PLURAL	-ae **nominative**	-ī **nom.**	nom.	nom.	nom.	nom.
	-ārum genitive	-ōrum gen.	gen.	gen.	gen.	gen.
	-īs dative	-īs dat.	dat.	dat.	dat.	dat.
	-ās accusative	-ōs acc.	acc.	acc.	acc.	acc.
	-īs ablative	-īs abl.	abl.	abl.	abl.	abl.

For more information on the first and second declensions, number, gender, and case, see pages 12-18 of Bennett's *New Latin Grammar* or pages 13-17 of Gildersleeve's *Latin Grammar*.

~~~~~~

Lesson 19

Pages 87-92 - Vocabulary and sentence practice - Part 3

****
QUIZ #2 (optional)
****

****
MIDTERM EXAM (optional)
****

Lesson 20
Pages 93-100 - New vocabulary - Part 3, vocabulary practice

> *English derivatives:*
> superō (superable, superably, insuperable, soubrette)
> cōpia (copy, copious, cornucopia)
> oppugnō (oppugn)
> vulnerō (vulnerable, vulnerability, vulnerably, vulnerableness,
> invulnerable)
> fuga (fugue, fugal, febrifuge, feverfew)
> temptō (tempt, tempter, temptable, temptation, attempt, attemptable,
> tentative, tentatively, tentativeness)
> servō (conserve, conservation, conservator, conservative, observe,
> observation, preserve, preservable, preservability, preservation,
> preservative, reserve, reservable, reservoir)
> poena (subpoena, pain, penal, penalty, penalize, penology, impunity,
> punish)

Lesson 21
Pages 101-106 - New vocabulary - Part 4, vocabulary practice

> *English derivatives:*
> semper (semipiternal, sempre)
> captīvus (captive, captivate, captivation, captivator, caitiff)
> locus (locus, local, localize, locale, locality, locally, allocate,
> allocation, locomotor, locomotion, locomotive, locate, dislocate,
> locule, loculus, milieu, lieu)
> audācia (audacity, audacious, audaciously)
> volō (volley, volatile, volatility, volitant, volant, Volans)
> animus (animus, unanimous, animosity, magnanimous, equanimity,
> pusillanimous, longanimity, animadvert)
> crās (procrastinate, procrastination)
> carrus (car, carry, cargo, caricature, chariot, charge, career, cariole,
> caroche)

Lesson 22
Pages 107-110 - Vocabulary practice

Lesson 23
Pages 111-116 - Vocabulary and sentence practice - Part 4

Lesson 24
Pages 117-120 - Second person - singular (first conjugation)

~~~~~~

The Big Picture - You Are Here

Conjugations (Verbs)					
MOOD **indicative** subjunctive imperative	**TENSE** **present** perfect imperfect pluperfect future future perfect			**VOICE** **active** passive	

	first conjugation		second conjugation	third conjugation	third i-stem conjugation	fourth conjugation	irregular
SINGULAR	-ā+ō=ō	1st person	1st	1st	1st	1st	1st
	-ā+s=ās	**2nd person**	2nd	2nd	2nd	2nd	2nd
	-ā+t=at	3rd person	3rd	3rd	3rd	3rd	3rd
PLURAL	-ā+mus=āmus	1st person	1st	1st	1st	1st	1st
	-ā+tis=ātis	2nd person	2nd	2nd	2nd	2nd	2nd
	-ā+nt=ant	3rd person	3rd	3rd	3rd	3rd	3rd

For more information on the first conjugation, see pages 58-61 of Bennett's *New Latin Grammar* or pages 72-75 of Gildersleeve's *Latin Grammar*.

~~~~~~

Lesson 25
Pages 121-124 - Ablative of "Place Where"

~~~~~~

The Big Picture - You Are Here

Special Case Uses (Ablative Case)		
showing separation	showing location	showing instrument or circumstances
place from which partitive place from which separation personal agent place from which (no preposition) cause comparison	**place where** time when time within which	means or instrument accompaniment manner description specification degree of difference ablative absolute

For more information on the special ablative case uses, see pages 146-151 of Bennett's *New Latin Grammar* or pages 246-265 of Gildersleeve's *Latin Grammar*.

~~~~~~

Lesson 25 (continued)

~~~~~~

Teacher tip:

On page 121, your student learns that the Latin preposition "in" can mean "in" or "on" when used with words ending in -ā or -ō. In Level 4, he will learn that "in" can mean "into" or "against" when used with other endings.

~~~~~~

Lesson 26

Pages 125-126 - Ablative of Means

~~~~~~

The Big Picture - You Are Here

Special Case Uses (Ablative Case)		
showing separation	showing location	showing instrument or circumstances
place from which partitive place from which separation personal agent place from which (no preposition) cause comparison	place where time when time within which	**means or instrument** accompaniment manner description specification degree of difference ablative absolute

For more information on the special ablative case uses, see pages 146-151 of Bennett's *New Latin Grammar* or pages 246-265 of Gildersleeve's *Latin Grammar*.

~~~~~~

~~~~~~

Teacher tip:

On page 125, the *by means of* construction is introduced. When your student wants to express in Latin that something is done *by means of* something else, he should use this construction. (This is called the *ablative of means or instrument* in Latin grammar. However, as stated earlier, your student need not be concerned about Latin terminology at this time. He simply needs to know the ending that is used to show the *means by which* something is done. In English, an example would be, "I summon the girls by means of the trumpet.")

If a noun is singular and ends in -a, that -a is lengthened (-ā) to show *by means of* (just as it was lengthened earlier when it followed the Latin preposition "in.") Likewise, if a noun is singular and ends in -us, that -us is changed to -ō to show *by means of* (just as it was changed earlier when it followed Latin "in." (See page 121 to review what happens to words ending in -a and -us when they follow the Latin preposition "in.")

If such a noun (whose singular form ends in -a or -us) is plural, the new ending is -īs in both instances. (See the bottom of page 123.)

Lesson 26 (continued)

As explained in the footnote on page 125, your student can use a variety of prepositions (such as "with," "in," or "on") in his translation as long as he remembers that the idea of this construction is "by means of."

~~~~~~

Lesson 27

Pages 127-128 - Ablative of Manner

~~~~~~

The Big Picture - You Are Here

Special Case Uses		
(Ablative Case)		
showing separation	showing location	showing instrument or circumstances
place from which partitive place from which separation personal agent place from which (no preposition) cause comparison	place where time when time within which	means or instrument accompaniment **manner** description specification degree of difference ablative absolute

For more information on the special ablative case uses, see pages 146-151 of Bennett's *New Latin Grammar* or pages 246-265 of Gildersleeve's *Latin Grammar*.

~~~~~~

Lesson 28

Pages 129-132 - Second person - plural (first conjugation)

~~~~~~

The Big Picture - You Are Here

Conjugations						
(Verbs)						
MOOD **indicative** subjunctive imperative		TENSE **present** perfect imperfect pluperfect future future perfect			VOICE **active** passive	
first conjugation		second conjugation	third conjugation	third i-stem conjugation	fourth conjugation	irregular
SINGULAR -ā+ō=ō	1st person	1st	1st	1st	1st	1st
-ā+s=ās	2nd person	2nd	2nd	2nd	2nd	2nd
-ā+t=at	3rd person	3rd	3rd	3rd	3rd	3rd
PLURAL -ā+mus=āmus	1st person	1st	1st	1st	1st	1st
-ā+tis=ātis	**2nd person**	2nd	2nd	2nd	2nd	2nd
-ā+nt=ant	3rd person	3rd	3rd	3rd	3rd	3rd

Lesson 28 (continued)

For more information on the first conjugation, see pages 58-61 of Bennett's *New Latin Grammar* or pages 72-75 of Gildersleeve's *Latin Grammar.*

~~~~~~

Lesson 29

Pages 133-136 - Dative case - singular (first and second declensions)

~~~~~~

The Big Picture - You Are Here

Declensions (Nouns)						
	first declension	**second declension**	third declension	third i-stem declension	fourth declension	fifth declension
	feminine **masculine**	**masculine** -us **masculine** -ius masculine -er neuter	masculine/ feminine neuter	masculine/ feminine neuter	masculine/ feminine neuter	masculine/ feminine
SINGULAR	-a nominative -ae genitive -ae **dative** -am accusative -ā ablative	-us nom. -ī gen. -ō **dat.** -um acc. -ō abl.	nom. gen. dat. acc. abl.	nom. gen. dat. acc. abl.	nom. gen. dat. acc. abl.	nom. gen. dat. acc. abl.
PLURAL	-ae nominative -ārum genitive -īs dative -ās accusative -īs ablative	-ī nom. -ōrum gen. -īs dat. -ōs acc. -īs abl.	nom. gen. dat. acc. abl.	nom. gen. dat. acc. abl.	nom. gen. dat. acc. abl.	nom. gen. dat. acc. abl.

For more information on the first and second declensions, number, gender, and case, see pages 12-18 of Bennett's *New Latin Grammar* or pages 13-17 of Gildersleeve's *Latin Grammar.*

~~~~~~

~~~~~~

Teacher tip:

The Latin verb "exspectō" means "I await" or "I wait for." Thus, the idea of "for" is contained in the meaning of the verb. It takes an *accusative* object. For example, "I wait for the daughter" would be translated "Filiam exspectō." (The *dative* case has various applications. The one your student is now learning is its use as an *indirect object.* That is, the word in the *dative* case shows that something is said, given, shown, or done "to" or "for" someone or something.)

~~~~~~

Lesson 30
Pages 137-140 - Dative case - plural (first and second declensions)

The Big Picture - You Are Here

Declensions (Nouns)					
first declension **feminine** **masculine**	**second declension** **masculine** -us **masculine** -ius masculine -er neuter	third declension masculine/feminine neuter	third i-stem declension masculine/feminine neuter	fourth declension masculine/feminine neuter	fifth declension masculine/feminine
SINGULAR -a nominative -ae genitive -ae dative -am accusative -ā ablative	-us nom. -ī gen. -ō dat. -um acc. -ō abl.	nom. gen. dat. acc. abl.	nom. gen. dat. acc. abl.	nom. gen. dat. acc. abl.	nom. gen. dat. acc. abl.
PLURAL -ae nominative -ārum genitive **-īs dative** -ās accusative -īs ablative	-ī nom. -ōrum gen. **-īs dat.** -ōs acc. -īs abl.	nom. gen. dat. acc. abl.	nom. gen. dat. acc. abl.	nom. gen. dat. acc. abl.	nom. gen. dat. acc. abl.

For more information on the first and second declensions, number, gender, and case, see pages 12-18 of Bennett's *New Latin Grammar* or pages 13-17 of Gildersleeve's *Latin Grammar*.

****
QUIZ #3 (optional)
****

Lesson 31
Pages 141-146 - New vocabulary - Part 5, vocabulary practice

English derivatives:
cūra (cure, secure, accurate, curious, curiosity, curio, curate, curator, curative, curacy, pedicure, manicure, procure, curette, sinecure, pococurante, scour)
stō (stay, state, stature, stance, stanch, stage, circumstance, contrast, distant, instant, instate, reinstate, constant, substance, obstacle, arrest, obstetric, institute, restive, restitute, extant, stator, stanchion, estancia, stet)
līberō (liberal, liberality, liberalize, liberate, liberator, deliver, livery)
interim (interim)
dēmōnstrō (demonstrate, demonstrator, demonstration, demonstrative, demonstrable)

Lesson 31 (continued)

> hōra (hour, horary)

Lesson 32

Pages 147-152 - New vocabulary - Part 6, vocabulary practice

English derivatives:
pecūnia (pecuniary, impecunious)
cōnfirmō (confirm, confirmable, confirmatory, confirmability)
clāmō (clamor, claim, acclaim, exclaim, reclaim, reclaimable,
    reclaimant, proclaim, proclamatory, disclaim, declaim, clamant,
    clamantly, quitclaim)
dominus (dominate, dominant, dominical, domineer, predominate,
    dominie, anno Domini, domain, dominion, domino, don, dame,
    damsel, madame, belladonna, madonna, dungeon, danger)
ambulō (amble, ambulate, ambulatory, ambulant, ambulance,
    preamble, perambulate, perambulation, perambulatory,
    noctambulist, noctambulism, somnambulist, funambulist,
    funambulism, ambulacrum, alley)
male (malefactor, malefaction, malevolence, maledict, maladroit,
    malformation, maladjusted, maladjustment, maladminister,
    malady, malapropism, malversation, malefic)
numerus (numerous, innumerous, number, numerable, numeral,
    numerical, numerate, enumerate, enumeration, enumerative,
    numerary, numerology, supernumerary)

Lesson 33

Pages 153-156 - Vocabulary practice

Lesson 34

Pages 157-160 - Sentence practice

Lesson 35

Pages 161-165 - Final review - Part 1

Lesson 36

Pages 166-170 - Final review - Part 2

****
QUIZ #4 (optional)
****

****
FINAL EXAM (optional)
****

Appendix

LET'S REVIEW THE LATIN ALPHABET

Ā ā

As you write the letters across each line, say the sound of "**a**" in *father*.

Ā ā Ā ā Ā ā Ā ā

As you write the letters across each line, say the sound of "**a**" in *idea*.

A a A a A a A a

A a

B b

As you write the letters across each line, say the sound of "**b**" in *boy*.

B b B b B b B b

As you write the letters across each line, say the sound of "**c**" in *cat*.

C c C c C c C c

C c

D̄ d̄

As you write the letters across each line, say the sound of "**d**" in *dog*.

D̄ d̄ D̄ d̄ D̄ d̄ D̄ d̄

As you write the letters across each line, say the sound of "**ey**" in *obey*.

Ē ē Ē ē Ē ē Ē ē

Ē ē

MORE LATIN ALPHABET REVIEW

As you write the letters across each line, say the sound of "e" in *bet*.

E e E e E e E e E e

E e

F f

As you write the letters across each line, say the sound of "f" in *fan*.

F f F f F f F f

As you write the letters across each line, say the sound of "g" in *go*.

G g G g G g G g

G g

H h

As you write the letters across each line, say the sound of "h" in *hat*.

H h H h H h H h

As you write the letters across each line, say the sound of "i" in *machine*.

Ī ī Ī ī Ī ī Ī ī

Ī ī

I i

As you write the letters across each line, say the sound of "i" in *sit*.

I i I i I i I i

MORE LATIN ALPHABET REVIEW

K k

As you write the letters across each line, say the sound of "**k**" in *king*.

K k K k K k K k

As you write the letters across each line, say the sound of "**l**" in *land*.

L l L l L l L l

L l

M m

As you write the letters across each line, say the sound of "**m**" in *man*.

M m M m M m M m

As you write the letters across each line, say the sound of "**n**" in *nut*.

N n N n N n N n

N n

Ō ō

As you write the letters across each line, say the sound of "**o**" in *note*.*

Ō ō Ō ō Ō ō Ō ō

As you write the letters across each line, say the sound of "**o**" in *omit*.*

O o O o O o O o

O o

*Although both Latin "o" sounds are "long," the ō as in *note* is held longer than the o as in *omit*.

MORE LATIN ALPHABET REVIEW

As you write the letters across each line, say the sound of **"p"** in *pit*.

P p P p P p P p

P p

Q q

As you write the letters across each line, say the sound of **"qu"** in *quit*.

Qu qu Qu qu

As you write the letters across each line, say the sound of **"r"** in *run*.

R r R r R r R r

R r

S s

As you write the letters across each line, say the sound of **"s"** in *sit*.

S s S s S s S s

As you write the letters across each line, say the sound of **"t"** in *tag*.

T t T t T t T t

T t

Ū ū

As you write the letters across each line, say the sound of **"u"** in *rule*.

Ū ū Ū ū Ū ū Ū ū

4

MORE LATIN ALPHABET REVIEW

As you write the letters across each line, say the sound of "**u**" in *put*.

As you write the letters across each line, say the sound of "**w**" in *way*.

As you write the letters across each line, say the sound of "**ks**" in *socks*.

As you write the letters across each line, form your lips to say "**oo**" but say "**ee**" instead. (Hold the sound longer than Latin y.)

As you write the letters across each line, form your lips to say "**oo**" but say "**ee**" instead. (Hold the sound shorter than Latin ȳ.)

As you write the letters across each line, say the sound of "**dz**" in *adze*.

MORE LATIN ALPHABET REVIEW

Match the letters to their sounds.

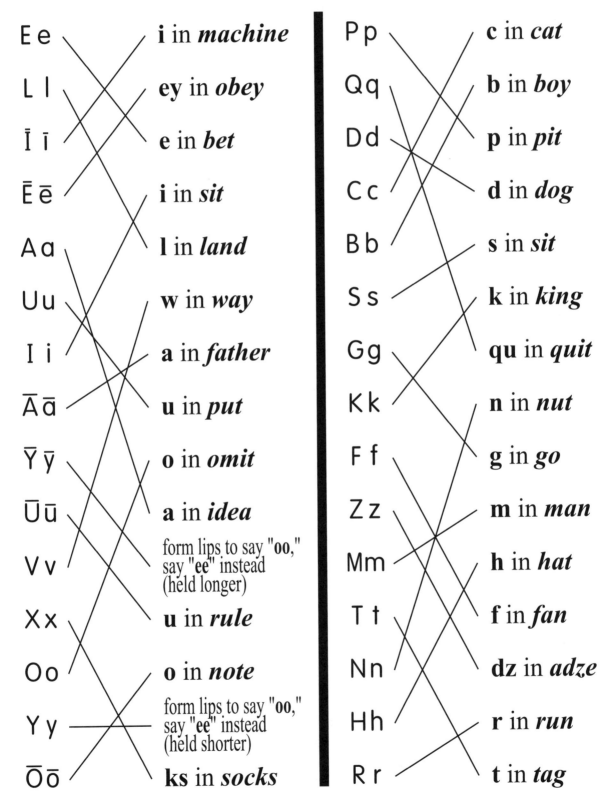

E e	i in *machine*
L l	ey in *obey*
Ī ī	e in *bet*
Ē ē	i in *sit*
A a	l in *land*
U u	w in *way*
I i	a in *father*
Ā ā	u in *put*
Ȳ ȳ	o in *omit*
Ū ū	a in *idea*
V v	form lips to say "oo," say "ee" instead (held longer)
X x	u in *rule*
O o	o in *note*
Y y	form lips to say "oo," say "ee" instead (held shorter)
Ō ō	ks in *socks*

P p	c in *cat*
Q q	b in *boy*
D d	p in *pit*
C c	d in *dog*
B b	s in *sit*
S s	k in *king*
G g	qu in *quit*
K k	n in *nut*
F f	g in *go*
Z z	m in *man*
M m	h in *hat*
T t	f in *fan*
N n	dz in *adze*
H h	r in *run*
R r	t in *tag*

6

LET'S REVIEW LATIN DIPHTHONGS

| ae | As you write the diphthong ae, say the "*aye*" sound. |

ae ae ae ae

As you write the diphthong au, say the "**ow**" sound in *now*.

au au au au

| | au |

| ei | As you write the diphthong ei, say the "**ei**" sound in *neighbor*. |

ei ei ei ei

As you write the diphthong eu, say "*ay-oo*" as one syllable.

eu eu eu eu

| | eu |

| oe | As you write the diphthong oe, say the "**oy**" sound in *joy*. |

oe oe oe oe

As you write the diphthong ui, say the "**uee**" sound in *queen*.

ui ui ui ui

| | ui |

MORE REVIEW

Color the ball and bat if the letters on the ball make the sound on the bat.

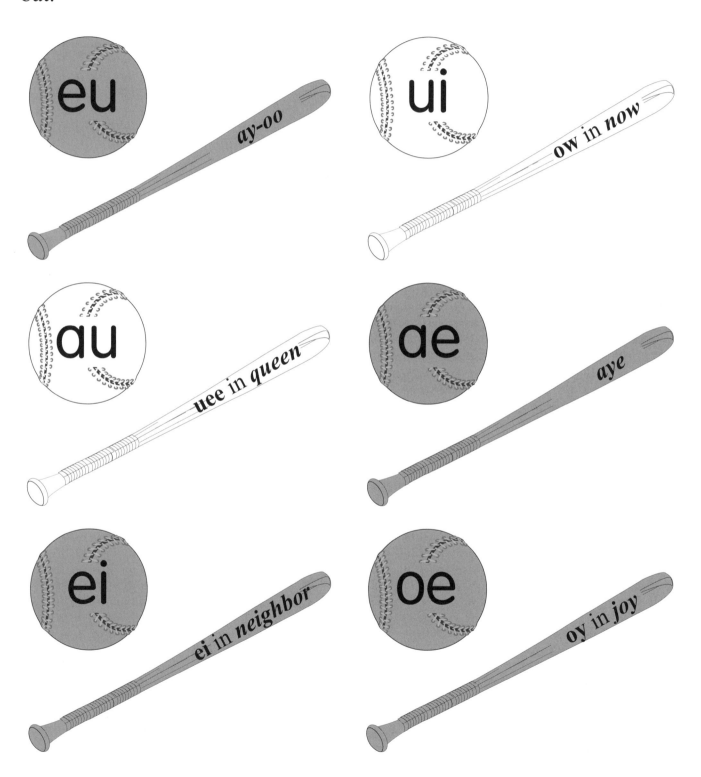

LET'S REVIEW SPECIAL CONSONANT SOUNDS

bs
As you write the consonants **bs**, say the "*ps*" sound.

bs   bs   bs   bs

As you write the consonants **bt**, say the "*pt*" sound.

bt

bt   bt   bt   bt

ch
As you write the consonants **ch**, say the "**ch**" sound in *character*.

ch   ch   ch   ch

As you write the consonants **gu**, say the "**gu**" sound in *anguish*.

gu

gu   gu   gu   gu

i
As you write the consonant **i**, say the "**y**" sound in *youth*.

i   i   i   i   i

As you write the consonants **ph**, say the "**ph**" sound in *phone*.

ph

ph   ph   ph   ph

su
As you write the consonants **su**, say the "**su**" sound in *suave*.

su   su   su   su

As you write the consonants **th**, say the "**th**" sound in *thick*.

th

th   th   th   th

MORE REVIEW

Write the Latin letters for each sound.

1. Latin **au** sounds like **ow** in *now*.

2. Latin **eu** sounds like **ay-oo** (in one syllable).

3. Latin **th** sounds like **th** in *thick*.

4. Latin **ph** sounds like **ph** in *phone*.

5. Latin **gu** sounds like **gu** in *anguish*.

6. Latin **su** sounds like **su** in *suave*.

7. Latin **bt** sounds like *pt*.

8. Latin **ui** sounds like **uee** in *queen*.

9. Latin **ch** sounds like **ch** in *character*.

10. Latin **i** sounds like **y** in *youth*.

11. Latin **ae** sounds like *aye*.

12. Latin **bs** sounds like *ps*.

10

VOCABULARY REVIEW

puella

means
girl

Write the Latin word that means **girl**.

puella

puella

Write the Latin word that means **I call**.

vocō

vocō

vocō

means
I call

puer

means
boy

Write the Latin word that means **boy**.

puer

puer

Write the Latin word that means **I give**.

dō

dō

dō

means
**I give,
I grant**

Start your flashcard deck with these cards. (See back of workbook.)
☐ I practiced my flashcards today.

VOCABULARY REVIEW

Write the Latin word that means **farmer**.

agricola

agricola

agricola
means
farmer

Write the Latin word that means **water**.

aqua
means
water

aqua

aqua

Write the Latin word that means **he is**.

est

est

est
means
he is, she is,
it is, there is

Write the Latin word that means **woman**.

fēmina
means
woman,
wife

fēmina

fēmina

☐ I practiced my flashcards today. (Add the new cards.)

Latin Workbook - Level 3
Copyright © 1998 by Karen Mohs

VOCABULARY REVIEW

et

means
**and, also,
even**

Write the Latin word that means **and**.

et

et

Write the Latin word that means **forest**.

silva

silva

silva

means
forest

īnsula

means
island

Write the Latin word that means **island**.

īnsula

īnsula

Write the Latin word that means **they are**.

sunt

sunt

sunt

means
**they are,
there are**

☐ I practiced my flashcards today. (Add the new cards.)

VOCABULARY REVIEW

Write the Latin word that means **I praise**.

laudō

laudō

laudō
means
I praise

nōn
means
not

Write the Latin word that means **not**.

nōn

nōn

Write the Latin word that means **to**.

ad

ad

ad
means
**to, near, toward,
for, at**

vīta
means
life

Write the Latin word that means **life**.

vīta

vīta

☐ I practiced my flashcards today. (Add the new cards.)

14

VOCABULARY REVIEW

porta
means
gate

Write the Latin word that means **gate**.

porta

porta

Write the Latin word that means **memory**.

memoria

memoria

memoria
means
memory

nāvigō
means
I sail

Write the Latin word that means **I sail**.

nāvigō

nāvigō

Write the Latin word that means **but**.

sed

sed

sed
means
but

☐ I practiced my flashcards today. (Add the new cards.)

VOCABULARY REVIEW

Write the Latin word that means **fortune**.

fortūna

fortūna

fortūna
means
**fortune,
chance, luck**

via
means
**road, way,
street**

Write the Latin word that means **way**.

via

via

Write the Latin word that means **I carry**.

portō

portō

portō
means
I carry

quid
means
what
(a question)

Write the Latin word that means **what?**

quid

quid

☐ I practiced my flashcards today. (Add the new cards.)

VOCABULARY REVIEW

tuba

means
trumpet

Write the Latin word that means **trumpet**.

tuba

tuba

Write the Latin word that means **field**.

ager

ager

ager

means
**field,
territory**

parō

means
**I prepare,
I prepare for**

Write the Latin word that means **I prepare**.

parō

parō

Write the Latin word that means **friend**.

amīcus

amīcus

amīcus

means
friend

☐ I practiced my flashcards today. (Add the new cards.)

VOCABULARY REVIEW

Write the Latin words.

I carry	portō	farmer	agricola
island	īnsula	he is	est
friend	amīcus	woman	fēmina
life	vīta	I give	dō
there are	sunt	I sail	nāvigō
not	nōn	but	sed
I prepare	parō	I call	vocō
territory	ager	even	et
toward	ad	memory	memoria
road	via	what?	quid
gate	porta	I praise	laudō
chance	fortūna	trumpet	tuba

☐ I practiced my flashcards today.

VOCABULARY REVIEW

spectō

means
I look at

Write the Latin word that means **I look at**.

spectō

spectō

Write the Latin word that means **nature**.

nātūra

nātūra

nātūra

means
nature

campus

means
**field,
plain**

Write the Latin word that means **field**.

campus

campus

Write the Latin word that means **I seize**.

occupō

occupō

occupō

means
**I seize,
I capture**

☐ I practiced my flashcards today. (Add the new cards.)

VOCABULARY REVIEW

Write the Latin word that means **with**.

cum
cum

| cum |
| means |
| **along with,** |
| **with** |

| nauta |
| means |
| **sailor** |

Write the Latin word that means **sailor**.

nauta
nauta

Write the Latin word that means **farmhouse**.

vīlla
vīlla

| vīlla |
| means |
| **farmhouse,** |
| **country house, villa** |

| littera |
| means |
| **letter** (of the alphabet), |
| (if plural: **epistle, letter**) |

Write the Latin word that means **letter**.

littera
littera

☐ I practiced my flashcards today. (Add the new cards.)

VOCABULARY REVIEW

ubi

means
where
(a question)

Write the Latin word that means **where?**

ubi

ubi

Write the Latin word that means **son**.

filius

filius

fīlius

means
son

patria

means
**country,
native land**

Write the Latin word that means **country**.

patria

patria

Write the Latin word that means **daughter**.

filia

filia

fīlia

means
daughter

☐ I practiced my flashcards today. (Add the new cards.)

VOCABULARY REVIEW

Write the Latin word that means **friendship**.

amīcitia

amīcitia

amīcitia

means
**friendliness,
friendship**

amō

means
**I love,
I like**

Write the Latin word that means **I love**.

amō

amō

Write the Latin word that means **tongue**.

lingua

lingua

lingua

means
**tongue,
language**

equus

means
horse

Write the Latin word that means **horse**.

equus

equus

☐ I practiced my flashcards today. (Add the new cards.)

VOCABULARY REVIEW

poēta
means
poet

Write the Latin word that means **poet**.

poēta

poēta

Write the Latin word that means **year**.

annus

annus

annus
means
year

pugnō
means
I fight

Write the Latin word that means **I fight**.

pugnō

pugnō

Write the Latin word that means **earth**.

terra

terra

terra
means
earth, land, country

☐ I practiced my flashcards today. (Add the new cards.)

VOCABULARY REVIEW

Write the Latin word that means **sword**.

gladius

gladius

gladius

means
sword

prōvincia

means
province

Write the Latin word that means **province**.

prōvincia

prōvincia

Circle **yes** or **no**.

yes   (no)   1. Aqua is a Latin word that means **blue**.

(yes)   no   2. Puer is a Latin word that means **boy**.

(yes)   no   3. Fortūna is a Latin word that means **luck**.

(yes)   no   4. Patria is a Latin word that means **country**.

yes   (no)   5. Tuba is a Latin word that means **straw**.

(yes)   no   6. Lingua is a Latin word that means **language**.

yes   (no)   7. Vīta is a Latin word that means **pill**.

yes   (no)   8. Nauta is a Latin word that means **bad**.

☐ I practiced my flashcards today. (Add the new cards.)

Latin Workbook - Level 3
Copyright © 1998 by Karen Mohs

VOCABULARY REVIEW

Match the words to their meanings.

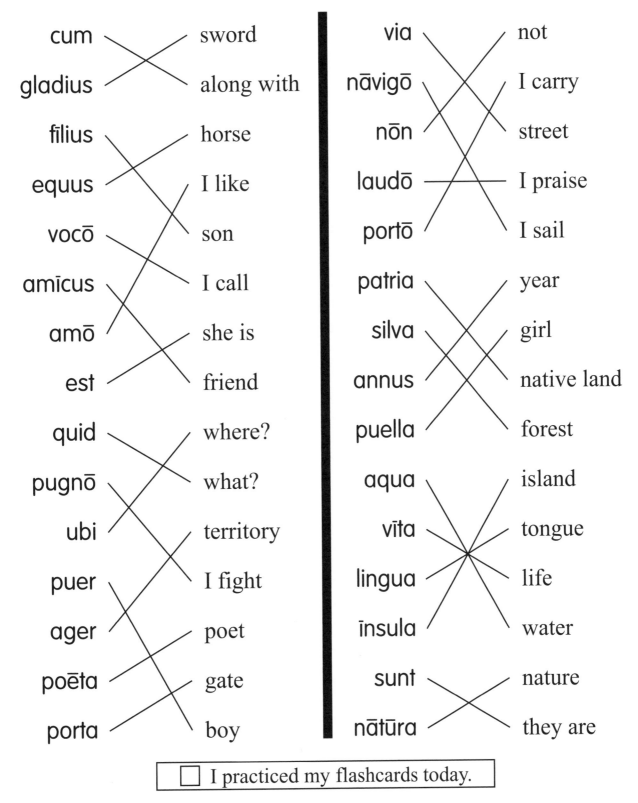

cum	sword
gladius	along with
filius	horse
equus	I like
vocō	son
amīcus	I call
amō	she is
est	friend

quid	where?
pugnō	what?
ubi	territory
puer	I fight
ager	poet
poēta	gate
porta	boy

via	not
nāvigō	I carry
nōn	street
laudō	I praise
portō	I sail

patria	year
silva	girl
annus	native land
puella	forest

aqua	island
vīta	tongue
lingua	life
īnsula	water

sunt	nature
nātūra	they are

☐ I practiced my flashcards today.

VOCABULARY REVIEW

Write the Latin words.

English	Latin	English	Latin
son	fīlius	poet	poēta
where?	ubi	sailor	nauta
girl	puella	friendship	amīcitia
plain	campus	nature	nātūra
earth	terra	year	annus
I look at	spectō	villa	vīlla
daughter	fīlia	horse	equus
sword	gladius	water	aqua
letter	littera	I fight	pugnō
language	lingua	with	cum
I love	amō	province	prōvincia
forest	silva	I seize	occupō

☐ I practiced my flashcards today.

Amō puellam.* It means **I like the girl.**

Amō fīlium. It means **I like the son.**

Now read these Latin sentences. Write what they mean.

1. Amō nautam.

   It means I like the sailor.

2. Amō vīllam.

   It means I like the farmhouse.

3. Spectō equum.

   It means I look at the horse.

4. Laudō amīcum.

   It means I praise the friend.

Put a check in the box when you notice:

☑ The last letters of the words fīlius, equus, and amīcus changed from us to um.

☑ The last letters of the words puella, nauta, and vīlla changed from a to am.

Endings of Latin words change when the words are used in different parts of the sentence. We will learn more about this later.

*This third level uses an *inductive* ("parts to whole") approach. See the paradigms in the appendix for the "whole" picture. Level Four transitions to a *deductive* ("whole to parts") approach.

☐ I practiced my flashcards today. (Add the new cards.)

LET'S PRACTICE

Circle the correct Latin words. Then write what the sentences mean.

1. Vocō (puellam.)
   puella.

   It means _I call the girl._

2. Gladius
   (Gladium) dō.*

   It means _I give the sword._

3. Pugnō agricola.
   (agricolam.)

   It means _I fight the farmer._

4. Parō (equum.)
   equus.

   It means _I prepare the horse._

Fill in the blanks with the correct Latin words.

1. _____ Spectō _____ campum.
   (I look at)

2. Portō _____ filiam _____.
   (the daughter)

3. _____ Silvam _____ occupō.
   (the forest)

*Notice that word order in Latin is not the same as word order in English. In Latin, since the ending tells us what part the word plays in the sentence, word order is used for emphasis. However, there is a tendency to place the verb last.

☐ I practiced my flashcards today.

LET'S PRACTICE

Choose the correct words for the sentences. Put them in the blanks.
Then write what the sentences mean.

| Fēminam - Fēmina | 1. **Fēminam** laudō. |

It means I praise the woman.

| tuba - tubam | 2. Spectō **tubam** . |

It means I look at the trumpet.

| Nauta - Nautam | 3. **Nautam** pugnō. |

It means I fight the sailor.

| Fīliam - Fīlia | 4. **Fīliam** portō. |

It means I carry the daughter.

| equus - equum | 5. Vocō **equum** . |

It means I call the horse.

| Aquam - Aqua | 6. **Aquam** amō. |

It means I like the water.

| Fīlius - Fīlium | 7. **Fīlium** occupō. |

It means I seize the son.

☐ I practiced my flashcards today.

LET'S PRACTICE

Connect each raindrop to the correct puddle.

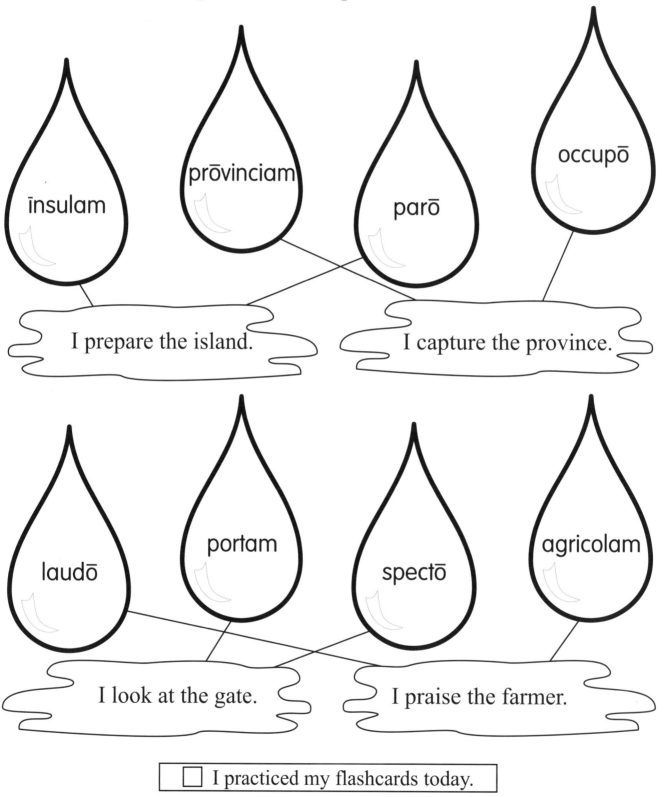

īnsulam

prōvinciam

parō

occupō

I prepare the island.

I capture the province.

laudō

portam

spectō

agricolam

I look at the gate.

I praise the farmer.

☐ I practiced my flashcards today.

Puellam amō.	It means **I like the girl.**
Puellās amō.	It means **I like the *girls*.**
Nautam amō.	It means **I like the sailor.**
Nautās amō.	It means **I like the *sailors*.**

Fill in the blanks with am or ās.

The ending __am__ changes to the ending __ās__ when the word means more than one.

Fīlium amō.	It means **I like the son.**
Fīliōs amō.	It means **I like the *sons*.**
Campum amō.	It means **I like the plain.**
Campōs amō.	It means **I like the *plains*.**

Fill in the blanks with um or ōs.

The ending __um__ changes to the ending __ōs__ when the word means more than one.

☐ I practiced my flashcards today. (Add the new cards.)

LET'S PRACTICE

Match the Latin sentences to their meanings.

_c_ 1. Gladiōs portō.   a. I love the daughters.

_a_ 2. Filiās amō.   b. I fight the poet.

_e_ 3. Vocō poētās.   c. I carry the swords.

_b_ 4. Poētam pugnō.   d. I like the friendship.

_d_ 5. Amō amīcitiam.   e. I call the poets.

_j_ 6. Terram occupō.   f. I prepare the way.

_i_ 7. Dō litterās.   g. I look at the letter.

_f_ 8. Viam parō.   h. I praise the native land.

_h_ 9. Patriam laudō.   i. I give the epistle.

_g_ 10. Litteram spectō.   j. I seize the land.

Circle the Latin sentence that means:

I love the sons and the friend.

1. Amō filius et amīcus.

2. (Filiōs et amīcum amō.)

3. Filiōs et amīcās amō.

☐ I practiced my flashcards today.

Latin Workbook - Level 3
Copyright © 1998 by Karen Mohs

LET'S PRACTICE

Write the sentences using the words on the right.

1. Tubās portō.

   It means **I carry the trumpets.**

2. Amīcōs spectō.

   It means **I look at friends.**

3. Vītam parō.

   It means **I prepare for life.**

amīcōs
parō
portō
spectō
tubās
vītam

Fill in the missing letters on the Latin words.

1. Agricol**am** voc**ō**, et amō fili**am**.

   It means **I call the farmer, and I like the daughter.**

2. Puell**ās** et gladi**ōs** laudō.

   It means **I praise the girls and the swords.**

3. D**ō** silv**ās**, et portō equ**ōs**.

   It means **I give the forests, and I carry the horses.**

☐ I practiced my flashcards today.

LET'S PRACTICE

Draw pictures for these sentences.

Puellam et gladiōs portō.

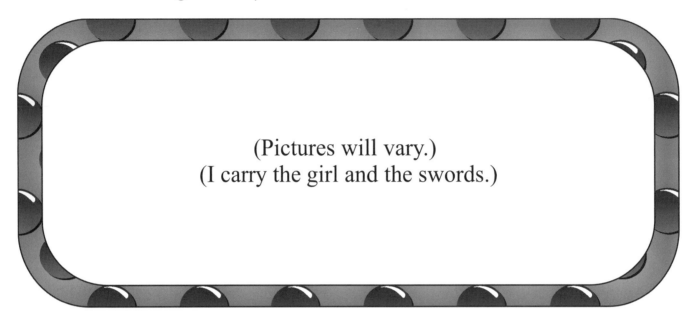

(Pictures will vary.)
(I carry the girl and the swords.)

Puellās et gladium portō.

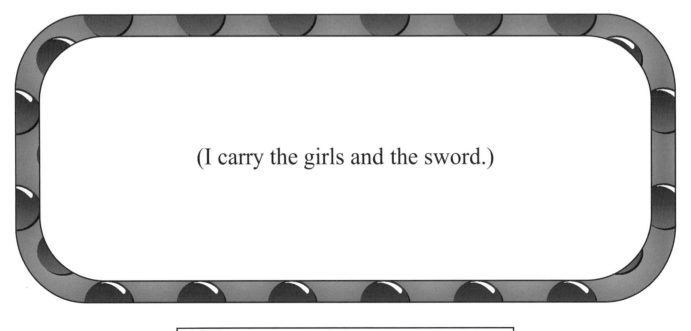

(I carry the girls and the sword.)

☐ I practiced my flashcards today.

Puellam amō.   It means **I like the girl.**
Puellam amāmus.   It means *We* **like the girl.**

Puellam portō.   It means **I carry the girl.**
Puellam portāmus.   It means *We* **carry the girl.**

Fill in the blank with either ō or āmus.

If I want to say *I* do something, I use the ending ___ō___.

If I want to say *we* do something, I use the ending _āmus_.

Match the Latin words to their meanings.

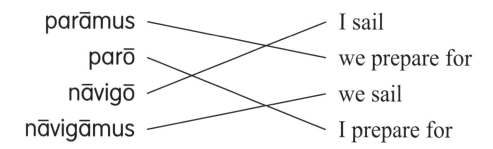

parāmus   I sail
parō   we prepare for
nāvigō   we sail
nāvigāmus   I prepare for

Read the Latin sentences. Write what they mean.

1. Occupāmus campōs, sed occupō viam.

   It means _We capture the plains, but I capture the road._

2. Pugnō poētam, et pugnāmus filiās.

   It means _I fight the poet, and we fight the daughters._

☐ I practiced my flashcards today. (Add the new cards.)

LET'S PRACTICE

Circle the correct Latin words.

I carry	memories
laudō portāmus parō (portō)	īnsulās equōs memoriam (memoriās)
fortunes	**life**
linguās fortūnam (fortūnās) prōvinciās	(vītam) vīllās vītās viās
we sail	**we love**
(nāvigāmus) nāvigō occupāmus portāmus	amō (amāmus) laudāmus occupō
nature	**I look at**
silvam nātūrās nautās (nātūram)	parō (spectō) spectāmus nāvigō
I call	**years**
vocāmus pugnō (vocō) laudāmus	patriam annum litteram (annōs)
friendliness	**I grant**
amīcitiās (amīcitiam) amīcum amīcōs	(dō) parāmus vocō laudō

☐ I practiced my flashcards today.

Latin Workbook - Level 3
 Copyright © 1998 by Karen Mohs

LET'S PRACTICE

Circle the correct meanings of the Latin sentences.

Silvās spectāmus.	I look at the forests. I look at the forest. (We look at the forests.)
Portō litterās.	You carry the epistle. (I carry the epistle.) We carry the epistle.
Puellās amō.	(I love the girls.) I love the girl. We love the girl.
Spectō vīllam.	We look at the farmhouse. I look at the farmhouses. (I look at the farmhouse.)
Portāmus portās.	You carry the gates. (We carry the gates.) I carry the gate.
Dō gladium.	(I give the sword.) He gives the sword. We give the swords.

☐ I practiced my flashcards today.

LET'S PRACTICE

Color the book blue if the word means only one. Color the book green if the word means more than one.

blue puellam

green tubās

green gladiōs

green terrās

green poētās

blue linguam

green patriās

blue campum

green filiōs

blue terram

green agricolās

green aquās

☐ I practiced my flashcards today.

Vīllam amō.

It means **I like the farmhouse.**

Vīllam puellae amō.

It means **I like the farmhouse *of the girl.***
or
I like the *girl's* farmhouse.

The new ending is ae. It replaces the a at the end of words like puella to show that the farmhouse belongs to the girl.

Vīllam filī amō.

It means **I like the farmhouse *of the son.***
or
I like the *son's* farmhouse.

Vīllam amīcī amō.

It means **I like the farmhouse *of the friend.***
or
I like the *friend's* farmhouse.

The new ending is ī. It replaces the ius at the end of words like filius (or the us at the end of words like amīcus) to show that the farmhouse belongs to the son (or to the friend).

Fill in the blank with either ae or ī to show something belongs.

If the word ends like puella, change the a to ___ae___.

If the word ends like filius, change the ius to ___ī___.

If the word ends like amīcus, change the us to ___ī___.

| ☐ I practiced my flashcards today. (Add the new cards.) |

LET'S PRACTICE

Circle the correct Latin words. Then write what the sentences mean.

1. Gladius
   (Gladiōs) nautae portō.

   It means I carry the sailor's swords.

2. Vocāmus (equuum) filī.
            equuus

   It means We call the son's horse.

3. Fīlia
   (Fīliam) fēminae pugnō.

   It means I fight the woman's daughter.

4. (Annōs) amīcitiae amāmus.
   Annus

   It means We love the years of friendliness.

Match the correct Latin sentences to their meanings below.

   a. Viās terrae laudō.   d. Nautās et agricolās vocō.

   b. Litterās poētae amō.   e. Nautās et agricolās vocāmus.

   c. Viās terrae spectāmus.   f. Litteram poētae dō.

  c   1. We look at the roads of the land.

  b   2. I love the poet's letter.

  a   3. I praise the roads of the land.

  e   4. We call the sailors and the farmers.

☐ I practiced my flashcards today.

LET'S PRACTICE

Choose the correct words for the sentences. Put them in the blanks.
Then write what the sentences mean.

| nautae - nauta |
1. Fīlium __nautae__ amāmus.

It means _We love the sailor's son._

| agricola - agricolae |
2. Pugnō equum __agricolae__.

It means _I fight the farmer's horse._

| tubam - tuba |
3. Portō puellae __tubam__.

It means _I carry the girl's trumpet._

| Silva - Silvam |
4. __Silvam__ fēminae occupāmus.

It means _We seize the woman's forest._

| patriae - patria |
5. Aquam laudāmus __patriae__.

It means _We praise the water of the country._

| Puella - Puellās |
6. __Puellās__ et fēminās vocō.

It means _I call the girls and the women._

| Gladius - Gladiōs |
7. __Gladiōs__ prōvinciae spectō.

It means _I look at the swords of the province._

| ☐ I practiced my flashcards today. |

LET'S PRACTICE

Draw a smile on the chef's face if the word on his hat matches the meaning on his bow tie. Draw a frown if the meanings do not match.

☐ I practiced my flashcards today.

lēgātus

means

lieutenant, envoy

Write the Latin word that means **envoy**.

lēgātus

lēgātus

lēgātus

Write the Latin word that means **game**.

lūdus

lūdus

lūdus

lūdus

means

game, play, school

appellō

means

I address, I call, I name

Write the Latin word that means **I address**.

appellō

appellō

appellō

☐ I practiced my flashcards today. (Add the new cards.)

LET'S PRACTICE

Color the box blue if the English meaning matches the Latin word at the beginning of the row.

cum	along with	I go	but
appellāmus	I name	we name	you name
lūdī	of the school	of schools	school
lēgātus	lieutenants	court	lieutenant
memoriās	of memories	memories	memory
appellō	he calls	I address	you name
lēgātī	courts	of the court	of the envoy
quid	what?	who?	why?
nāvigāmus	they sail	she sails	we sail
nātūrās	natures	shoes	beauty

☐ I practiced my flashcards today.

servus

means

slave

Write the Latin word that means **slave**.

servus

servus

servus

Write the Latin word that means **message**.

nūntius

nūntius

nūntius

nūntius

means

messenger, message, news

nūntiō

means

I announce, I report

Write the Latin word that means **I report**.

nūntiō

nūntiō

nūntiō

☐ I practiced my flashcards today. (Add the new cards.)

LET'S PRACTICE

Circle the correct Latin words.

we prepare for		of the memory	
pugnāmus	patriās	īnsula	vīta
portāmus	(parāmus)	equī	(memoriae)
messengers		**I praise**	
nātūrae	poētam	(laudō)	lēgātōs
(nūntiōs)	nautam	linguam	lēgātum
of the water		**I grant**	
(aquae)	amīcitiae	gladī	(dō)
annī	amīcum	fortūnae	portam
message		**year**	
(nūntium)	nātūra	amīcī	(annum)
memoria	nūntī	amāmus	terram
we report		**language**	
parō	nūntius	(lingua)	lūdum
(nūntiāmus)	nūntiō	lūdus	littera
of the slave		**schools**	
servum	servus	(lūdōs)	linguae
(servī)	servōs	litterae	campum

☐ I practiced my flashcards today.

nārrō

means

**I relate,
I tell**

Write the Latin word that means **I relate**.

nārrō

nārrō

nārrō

Write the Latin word that means **rumor**.

fāma

fāma

fāma

fāma

means

**report, rumor,
reputation**

populus*

means

**people, nation,
tribe**

Write the Latin word that means **people**.

populus

populus

populus

*Populus is usually singular. If plural, it means *nations* or *tribes*.

☐ I practiced my flashcards today. (Add the new cards.)

LET'S PRACTICE

Choose the correct words for the sentences. Put them in the blanks.
Then write what the sentences mean.

| populī - populus | 1. Memoriam nārrō ___populī___.
It means _I tell the memory of the people._ |

| fāmās - fāmae | 2. Nūntiāmus ___fāmās___ servī.
It means _We report the rumors of the slave._ |

| viae - viam | 3. Vīllam et ___viam___ spectāmus.
It means _We look at the farmhouse and the road._ |

| Populum - Populus | 4. ___Populum___ nūntī pugnō.
It means _I fight the people of the messenger._ |

| fortūna - fortūnās | 5. Fīliae ___fortūnās___ nārrāmus.
It means _We tell the fortunes of the daughter._ |

| īnsula - īnsulae | 6. Poētās ___īnsulae___ amō.
It means _I love the poets of the island._ |

| lēgātī - lēgātōs | 7. Fīliōs appellāmus ___lēgātī___.
It means _We address the sons of the envoy._ |

☐ I practiced my flashcards today.

48

rēgīna

means

queen

Write the Latin word that means **queen**.

rēgīna

rēgīna

rēgīna

Write the Latin word that means **I await**.

exspectō

exspectō

exspectō

exspectō

means

**I await,
I wait for**

epistula

means

**letter,
epistle**

Write the Latin word that means **letter**.

epistula

epistula

epistula

☐ I practiced my flashcards today. (Add the new cards.)

LET'S PRACTICE

Write the meanings of these Latin words.

Latin	Meaning	Latin	Meaning
servī	of the slave	rēgīnam	queen
fīliam	daughter	silvās	forests
exspectō	I await, I wait for	patria	country, native land
tubās	trumpets	occupō	I seize, I capture
vītās	lives	nātūrae	of nature
populus	people, nation, tribe	lūdus	game, play, school
epistula	letter, epistle	fāma	report, rumor, reputation
rēgīnae	of the queen	amīcōs	friends
vocāmus	we call	amāmus	we love, we like
tubam	trumpet	nātūram	nature
parāmus	we prepare, we prepare for	terra	earth, land, country
campōs	fields, plains	damus	we give, we grant
rēgīnās	queens	puellam	girl
patriam	country, native land	silvae	of the forest
gladī	of the sword	īnsulās	islands

☐ I practiced my flashcards today.

Latin Workbook - Level 3
Copyright © 1998 by Karen Mohs

habitō

means

I live,
I dwell

Write the Latin word that means **I live**.

habitō

habitō

habitō

Write the Latin word that means **now**.

nunc

nunc

nunc

nunc

means

now

fābula

means

story

Write the Latin word that means **story**.

fābula

fābula

fābula

☐ I practiced my flashcards today. (Add the new cards.)

LET'S PRACTICE

Color the box green if the Latin word matches the English meaning at the beginning of the row.

I wait for	specto	appello	**exspecto**
of the nation	**populi**	populos	populus
story	fabulas	**fabula**	fabulae
island	**insulam**	insulae	insulas
we dwell	narramus	habito	**habitamus**
province	**provincia**	provinciae	provincias
reputations	fama	**famas**	famam
of the letter	epistulas	epistula	**epistulae**
now	**nunc**	non	ad
of the year	annos	**anni**	annus

I practiced my flashcards today.

52

dēlectō

means

I please

Write the Latin word that means **I please**.

dēlectō

dēlectō

dēlectō

Write the Latin word that means **I labor**.

labōrō

labōrō

labōrō

labōrō

means

**I labor, I suffer,
I am hard pressed**

---

causa

means

**cause,
reason**

Write the Latin word that means **cause**.

causa

causa

causa

☐ I practiced my flashcards today. (Add the new cards.)

LET'S PRACTICE

Write the Latin words.

but	sed	of the language	linguae
villas	vīllās	daughters	fīliās
now	nunc	I tell	nārrō
of the story	fābulae	of the street	viae
tribes	populōs	we carry	portāmus
lives	vītās	with	cum
of the poet	poētae	of the earth	terrae
I please	dēlectō	swords	gladiōs
I suffer	labōrō	of the queen	rēgīnae
of the horse	equī	years	annōs
gates	portās	of the water	aquae
causes	causās	where?	ubi

☐ I practiced my flashcards today.

socius

means

comrade, ally

Write the Latin word that means **ally**.

socius

socius

socius

Write the Latin word that means **care**.

dīligentia

dīligentia

dīligentia

dīligentia

means

diligence, care

convocō

means

I call together, I assemble, I summon

Write the Latin word that means **I summon**.

convocō

convocō

convocō

☐ I practiced my flashcards today. (Add the new cards.)

LET'S PRACTICE

Match the words to their meanings.

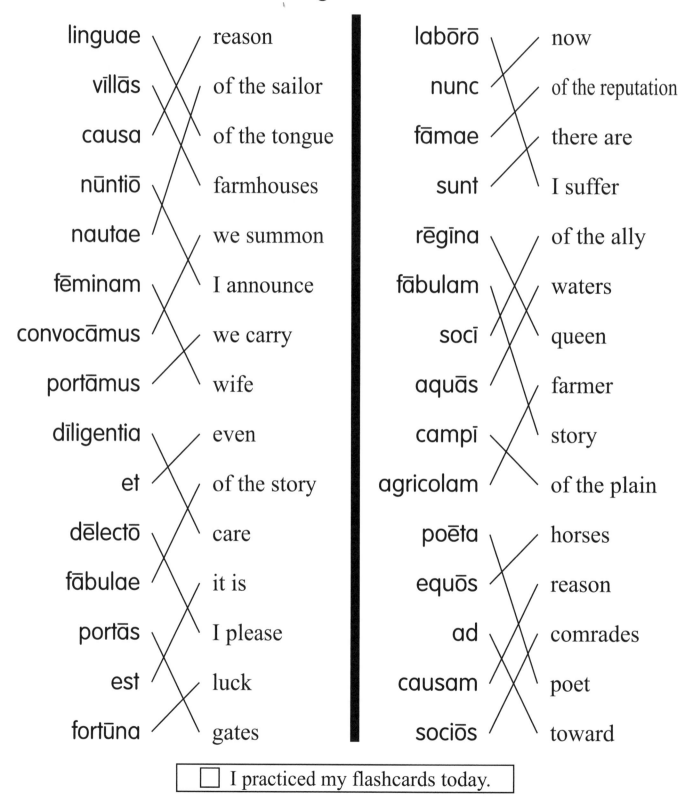

linguae	reason
vīllās	of the sailor
causa	of the tongue
nūntiō	farmhouses
nautae	we summon
fēminam	I announce
convocāmus	we carry
portāmus	wife
dīligentia	even
et	of the story
dēlectō	care
fābulae	it is
portās	I please
est	luck
fortūna	gates

labōrō	now
nunc	of the reputation
fāmae	there are
sunt	I suffer
rēgina	of the ally
fābulam	waters
socī	queen
aquās	farmer
campī	story
agricolam	of the plain
poēta	horses
equōs	reason
ad	comrades
causam	poet
sociōs	toward

☐ I practiced my flashcards today.

56

LET'S PRACTICE

Write the Latin words.

comrade	socius
I await	exspectō
way	via
game	lūdus
message	nūntius
now	nunc
rumor	fāma
I labor	labōrō
cause	causa
I report	nūntiō
but	sed
I summon	convocō

story	fābula
I name	appellō
envoy	lēgātus
I please	dēlectō
queen	rēgīna
with	cum
I relate	nārrō
people	populus
I prepare	parō
slave	servus
diligence	dīligentia
I dwell	habitō

☐ I practiced my flashcards today.

LET'S PRACTICE

Color the light bulb yellow if the word on the bulb and on the base mean the same.

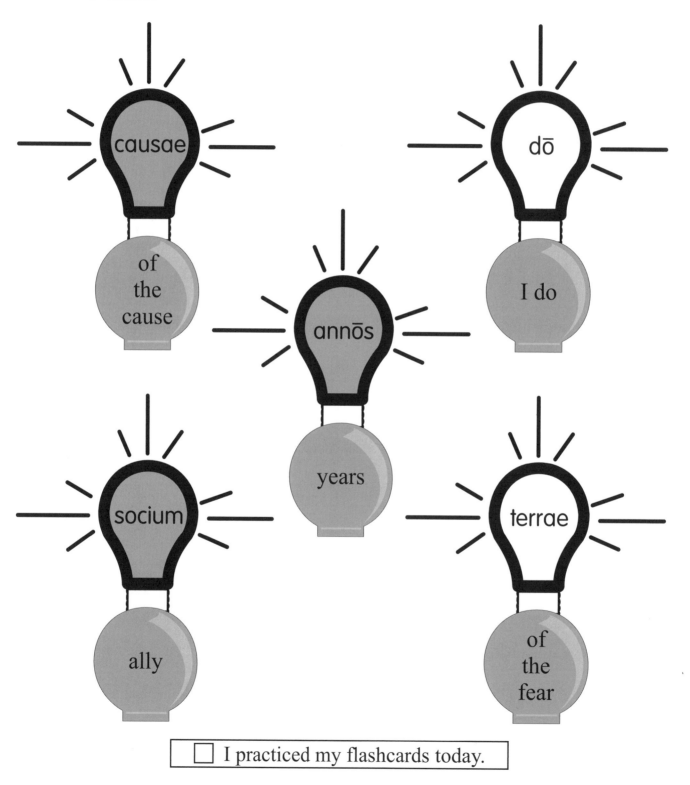

☐ I practiced my flashcards today.

LET'S PRACTICE

Write these sentences in Latin.

1. I praise the friendliness of the poet.

Amīcitiam poētae laudō.

2. We please the nations of the son.

Fīlī populōs dēlectāmus.

3. I tell the wife's stories.

Nārrō fābulās fēminae.

Circle the correct meanings.

populus	(people)	city	number
fābula	fashion	(story)	cable
rēgina	(queen)	king	kingdom
fāma	star	hunger	(report)
socius	directory	(comrade)	party

☐ I practiced my flashcards today.

LET'S PRACTICE

Color the apple brown if the word on the apple and the word on the worm mean the same.

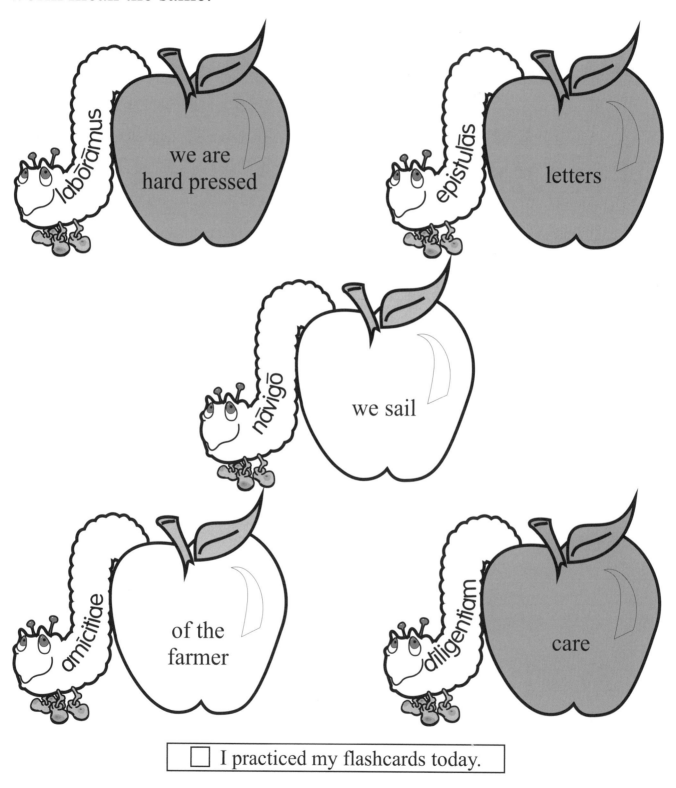

laborāmus	we are hard pressed
epistulās	letters
nāvigō	we sail
amīcitiae	of the farmer
dīligentiam	care

☐ I practiced my flashcards today.

60

LET'S PRACTICE

Match the Latin sentences to their meanings.

_e_ 1. Causās nūntiāmus.   a. We seize the province.

_c_ 2. Vītam amō.   b. We wait for the people.

_a_ 3. Prōvinciam occupāmus.   c. I love life.

_d_ 4. Fīliās spectō.   d. I look at the daughters.

_b_ 5. Exspectāmus populum.   e. We report the causes.

_h_ 6. Amīcī vocō fīlium.   f. I call together the poets.

_f_ 7. Poētās convocō.   g. I seize the messenger.

_i_ 8. Spectāmus lūdōs equī.   h. I call the friend's son.

_j_ 9. Terrās pugnō rēgīnae.   i. We look at the horse's games.

_g_ 10. Occupō nūntium.   j. I fight the queen's countries.

_n_ 11. Sociōs fīlī pugnāmus.   k. I carry the sword.

_o_ 12. Prōvinciās dō.   l. I tell the girl's stories.

_k_ 13. Gladium portō.   m. We praise the friendships.

_m_ 14. Laudāmus amīcitiās.   n. We fight the son's allies.

_l_ 15. Fābulās puellae nārrō.   o. I grant provinces.

☐ I practiced my flashcards today.

LET'S PRACTICE

Write the meanings of these Latin sentences.

1. Īnsulam et silvam terrae appellāmus.

   It means <u>We name the island and the forest of the country.</u>

2. Fābulam nūntiō, sed fāmam nōn nūntiō.

   It means <u>I report the story, but I do not report the rumor.</u>

3. Lēgātum et equum servī nunc laudō.

   It means <u>Now I praise the lieutenant and the slave's horse.</u>

4. Rēgīnās exspectāmus, sed populōs nōn exspectāmus.

   It means <u>We await the queens, but we do not await the nations.</u>

5. Viās parō et portās et vīllās.

   It means <u>I prepare the roads and the gates and the farmhouses.</u>

Choose the correct words for the sentences. Put them in the blanks.
Then write what the sentences mean.

| patriae - patria | 1. Agricolās **patriae** dēlectāmus. |

It means <u>We please the farmers of the native land.</u>

| Tubae - Tubam | 2. **Tubam** exspectō agricolae. |

It means <u>I await the farmer's trumpet.</u>

| Nautās - Nauta | 3. **Nautās** prōvinciae convocāmus. |

It means <u>We assemble the sailors of the province.</u>

☐ I practiced my flashcards today.

LET'S PRACTICE

Fill in the missing letters on the Latin words.

1. Gladi**um** port**ō**, et lēgāt**um** pugn**ō**.
   It means **I carry the sword, and I fight the lieutenant.**

2. Nāvig**āmus**, et spectāmus īnsul**ās** rēginae.
   It means **We sail, and we look at the queen's islands.**

3. Patri**am** naut**ae** am**āmus**.
   It means **We love the native land of the sailor.**

Match the words to their meanings.

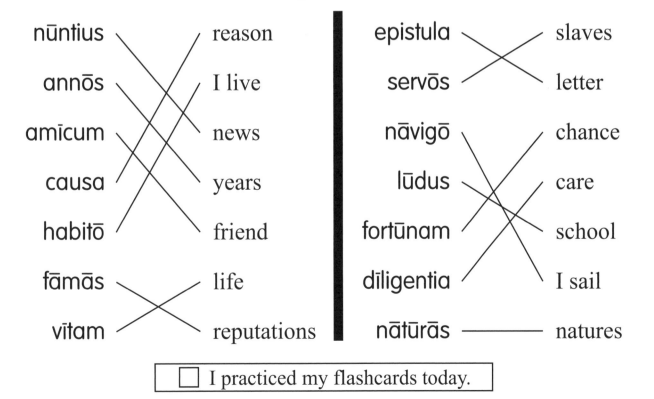

nūntius	reason	epistula	slaves
annōs	I live	servōs	letter
amīcum	news	nāvigō	chance
causa	years	lūdus	care
habitō	friend	fortūnam	school
fāmās	life	dīligentia	I sail
vītam	reputations	nātūrās	natures

☐ I practiced my flashcards today.

LET'S PRACTICE

Draw a line from each noodle to the correct soup kettle.

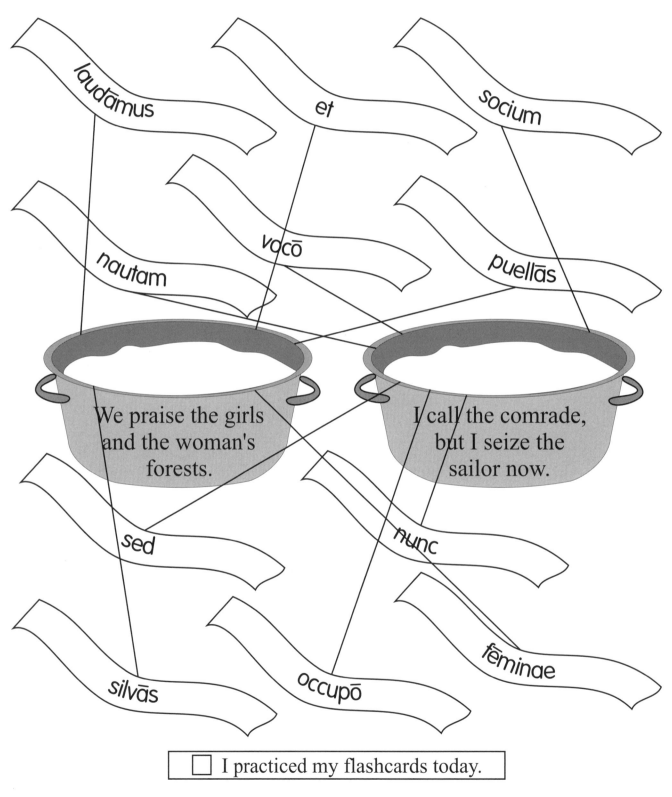

laudāmus

et

socium

vocō

nautam

puellās

We praise the girls and the woman's forests.

I call the comrade, but I seize the sailor now.

sed

nunc

silvās

occupō

fēminae

I practiced my flashcards today.

LET'S PRACTICE

Fill in the blanks with the correct words from the boxes on the right. Then write the meanings of the sentences.

1. Servum **lēgātī** vocāmus.

   It means We call the slave of the lieutenant.

   | socius |
   | lēgātī |
   | exspectō |

2. Poētam et fēminam **appellō**.

   It means I name the poet and the woman.

   | appellō |
   | lūdus |
   | via |

3. Tubās et **gladiōs** parāmus.

   It means We prepare the trumpets and the swords.

   | sed |
   | labōrō |
   | gladiōs |

4. **Amō** nunc rēginam populī.

   It means Now I like the queen of the people.

   | Cum |
   | Nōn |
   | Amō |

5. Aquās **īnsulae** nōn occupāmus.

   It means We do not capture the island's waters.

   | nūntiō |
   | īnsulae |
   | populus |

6. Dēlectō filiās et **fēminās**.

   It means I please the daughters and the wives.

   | fēminās |
   | parō |
   | fābula |

7. **Epistulās** poētae spectō.

   It means I look at the epistles of the poet.

   | Dīligentia |
   | Epistulās |
   | Habitō |

☐ I practiced my flashcards today.

LET'S PRACTICE

Draw pictures for these sentences.

Causās nārrāmus, sed gladiōs socī nōn portāmus.

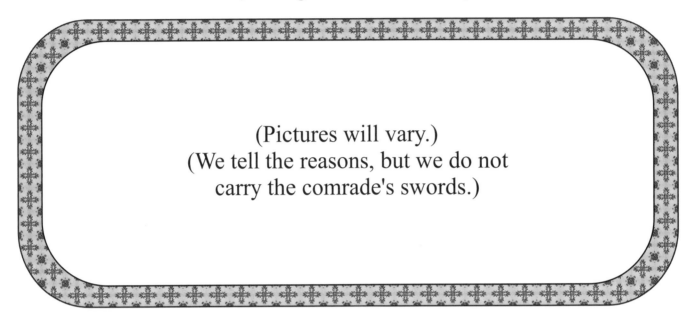

(Pictures will vary.)
(We tell the reasons, but we do not
carry the comrade's swords.)

Causās nārrō, sed gladium socī nōn portō.

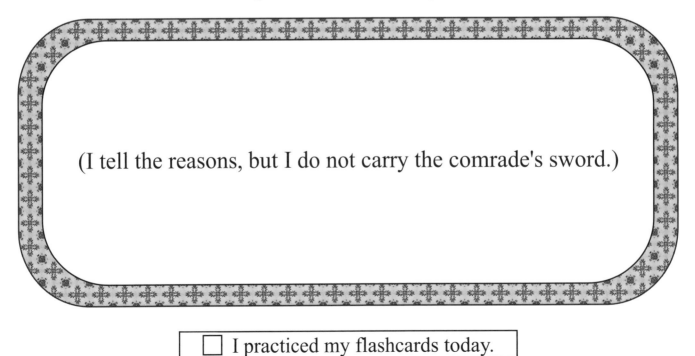

(I tell the reasons, but I do not carry the comrade's sword.)

☐ I practiced my flashcards today.

Vīllam puellae amō.
It means **I like the farmhouse** *of the girl.*
or
I like the *girl's* **farmhouse.**

Vīllam puellārum amō.
It means **I like the farmhouse** *of the girls.*
or
I like the *girls'* **farmhouse.**

The new ending is ārum. Just as ae at the end of words like puella shows that the farmhouse belongs to the girl, ārum shows it belongs to more than one girl.

Vīllam filiōrum* amō.
It means **I like the farmhouse** *of the sons.*
or
I like the *sons'* **farmhouse.**

Vīllam amīcōrum amō.
It means **I like the farmhouse** *of the friends.*
or
I like the *friends'* **farmhouse.**

The new ending is ōrum. It replaces the us at the end of words like filius or amīcus to show that the farmhouse belongs to more than one son (or more than one friend).

Circle the words that mean belonging to more than one son or friend.

(filiōrum)   filōrum   amīciōrum   (amīcōrum)

*Careful. Don't forget to keep the i if the word normally ends in ius. Notice the difference. As we learned on page 39, *singular* words, when used to show possession, do ***not*** keep the i before the ī ending (e.g. filī).

☐ I practiced my flashcards today. (Add the new cards.)

LET'S PRACTICE

Fill in the blanks with the correct Latin words.

1. Epistulam _____ **agricolae** _____ exspectō.
(of the farmer)

2. Patriam pugnāmus _____ **lēgātōrum** _____ .
(of the lieutenants)

3. Memoriās _____ **fīliārum** _____ nūntiō.
(of the daughters)

4. Amīcōs _____ **poētārum** _____ laudāmus.
(of the poets)

Match the Latin words to their meanings.

_b_ 1. patriārum   a. of the horse

_f_ 2. nautae   b. of the native lands

_c_ 3. patriae   c. of the native land

_g_ 4. equōrum   d. of the sailors

_a_ 5. equī   e. of the messengers

_d_ 6. nautārum   f. of the sailor

_e_ 7. nūntiōrum   g. of the horses

☐ I practiced my flashcards today.

LET'S PRACTICE

Write the Latin words.

of the wives	fēminārum	of the sword	gladī
of the water	aquae	of the years	annōrum
of the life	vītae	of the sons	filiōrum
of the forests	silvārum	of the friend	amīcī
of the message	nūntī	of the allies	sociōrum
of the schools	lūdōrum	of the way	viae

Circle **yes** or **no**.

(yes) no 1. Latin puellārum means **of the girls**.

yes (no) 2. Latin filiae means **of the daughters**.

yes (no) 3. Latin gladiōrum means **of the sword**.

(yes) no 4. Latin lūdī means **of the school**.

yes (no) 5. Latin silvae means **of the forests**.

(yes) no 6. Latin amīcōrum means **of the friends**.

(yes) no 7. Latin fābulae means **of the story**.

yes (no) 8. Latin vīllārum means **of the country house**.

☐ I practiced my flashcards today.

LET'S PRACTICE

Circle the correct Latin words. Then write what the sentences mean.

1. Prōvinciam et campōs (agricolārum) / agricola occupāmus.

   It means We seize the province and the plains of the farmers.

2. Portō memoriam (puellae) / puella.

   It means I carry the memory of the girl.

3. (Linguam) / Lingua et lūdum (populōrum) / populus appellō.

   It means I name the language and the school of the tribes.

4. (Fīliōs) / Fīlius et equōs fīliōrum convocāmus.

   It means We summon the sons and the horses of the sons.

5. Dīligentia / (Dīligentiam) servōrum nōn pugnāmus.

   It means We do not fight the slaves' diligence.

6. Aqua / (Aquam) spectō, et nātūram amō.

   It means I look at the water, and I love nature.

7. Litterās (fīlī) / fīlius et nūntiōs terra / (terrārum) exspectāmus.

   It means We await the son's letter and the countries' messages.

8. Laudō amīcitiam (rēgīnārum) / regina, sed rēgīnās nōn laudō.

   It means I praise the queens' friendliness, but I do not praise the queens.

9. (Vīllam) / Vīlla parāmus, et fīlia / (fīliam) vocāmus.

   It means We prepare the villa, and we call the daughter.

☐ I practiced my flashcards today.

Puellam amō.   It means **I like the girl.**

Puellam amat.   It means *He (she or it)* **likes the girl.**

Puellam portō.   It means **I carry the girl.**

Puellam portat.   It means *He (she or it)* **carries the girl.**

Fill in the blank with ō or āmus or at.

If I want to say *I* do something, I use the ending ___ō___.

If I want to say *we* do something, I use the ending _āmus_.

If I want to say *he* does something, I use the ending ___at___.

Match the Latin words to their meanings.

__e__ 1. nāvigāmus   a. she sails

__c__ 2. labōrō   b. I sail

__g__ 3. dat   c. I am hard pressed

__a__ 4. nāvigat   d. he is hard pressed

__f__ 5. labōrāmus   e. we sail

__b__ 6. nāvigō   f. we are hard pressed

__d__ 7. labōrat   g. it gives

☐ I practiced my flashcards today. (Add the new cards.)

LET'S PRACTICE

Draw lines from the Latin sentences to their meanings.

Lēgātōs prōvinciārum vocō.   We call the provinces' envoys.

Lēgātōs prōvinciārum vocāmus.   I call the provinces' envoys.

Lēgātōs prōvinciārum vocat.   He calls the provinces' envoys.

Equōs agricolārum exspectat.   She awaits the farmers' horses.

Equōs agricolārum exspectō.   We await the farmers' horses.

Equōs agricolārum exspectāmus.   I await the farmers' horses.

Nārrō dīligentiās puellae.   We relate the girl's cares.

Nārrat dīligentiās puellae.   I relate the girl's cares.

Nārrāmus dīligentiās puellae.   She relates the girl's cares.

Portam vīllae spectat.   I look at the villa's gate.

Portam vīllae spectāmus.   We look at the villa's gate.

Portam vīllae spectō.   He looks at the villa's gate.

Fēminās īnsulārum dēlectāmus.   It pleases the islands' wives.

Fēminās īnsulārum dēlectō.   We please the islands' wives.

Fēminās īnsulārum dēlectat.   I please the islands' wives.

☐ I practiced my flashcards today.

Latin Workbook - Level 3
Copyright © 1998 by Karen Mohs

LET'S PRACTICE

Write the meanings on the lines below the Latin sentences.

Nautās pugnat.	Gladiōs portāmus.
He* fights the sailors.	We carry the swords.
Nautam pugnō.	Gladium portat.
I fight the sailor.	He carries the sword.
Nūntium parat.	Fābulās nūntiat.
He prepares the message.	He reports the stories.
Nūntiōs parāmus.	Fābulam nūntiāmus.
We prepare the messages.	We report the story.
Populōs convocat.	Sociōs appellāmus.
He summons the tribes.	We name the allies.
Populum convocō.	Socium appellat.
I summon the tribe.	He names the ally.

Choose the correct words for the sentences. Put them in the blanks.
Then write what the sentences mean.

| sed - laudat | 1. Viam et campum __laudat__. |

It means __He praises the street and the plain.__

| amat - nunc | 2. Puellam nōn __amat__. |

It means __He does not like the girl.__

*Although the answer given uses the pronoun *he*, the pronouns *she* and *it* are correct as well. Follow this pattern through the remainder of this workbook.

☐ I practiced my flashcards today.

LET'S PRACTICE

Color the muffin brown if the words inside mean the same.

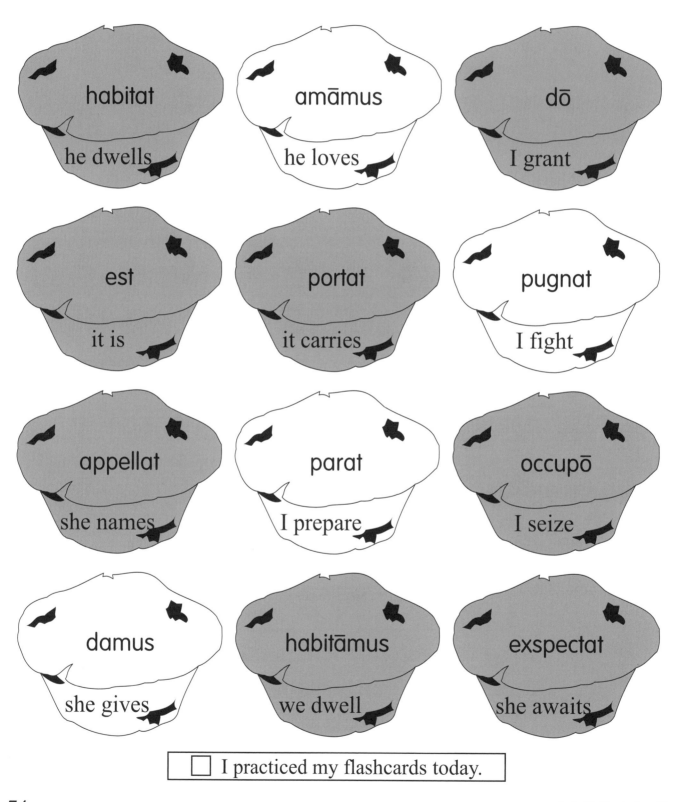

habitat / he dwells	amāmus / he loves	dō / I grant
est / it is	portat / it carries	pugnat / I fight
appellat / she names	parat / I prepare	occupō / I seize
damus / she gives	habitāmus / we dwell	exspectat / she awaits

☐ I practiced my flashcards today.

Puellam amat.

It means **He likes the girl.**

Now let's use a word that tells us who *he* is.

Let's use *the farmer*.

Agricola puellam amat.

It means **The farmer likes the girl.**

Fill in the blanks with the correct words from the boxes on the right. Then write the meanings of the sentences.

1. **Lēgātus** gladium spectat.

   It means The lieutenant looks at the sword.

   | Lēgātōs |
   | Lēgātus |
   | Lēgātum |

2. **Poēta** fābulās nārrat.

   It means The poet tells the stories.

   | Poēta |
   | Poētam |
   | Poētās |

3. **Fīlia** amīcōs convocat.

   It means The daughter assembles the friends.

   | Fīliās |
   | Fīlia |
   | Fīliam |

4. **Fīlius** īnsulam occupat.

   It means The son captures the island.

   | Fīliōs |
   | Fīlium |
   | Fīlius |

☐ I practiced my flashcards today.

LET'S PRACTICE

Fill in the blanks with the correct Latin words.

1. **Parō** _____ viās, sed nōn parō equōs.
(I prepare)

2. Fīliōs et fīliās **rēginae** _____ exspectāmus.
(of the queen)

3. **Agricola** _____ fāmam poētārum nōn nūntiat.
(the farmer)

4. Portās et viās vīllārum nunc **spectāmus** _____ .
(we look at)

5. **Puella** _____ fīlium lēgātī et fēminae portat.
(the girl)

6. **Servus** _____ lēgātum dēlectat, sed rēginam nōn dēlectat.
(the slave)

7. **Amīcōs** _____ et sociōs fēminārum laudō.
(the friends)

8. Amīcus socium et equum **agricolae** _____ vocat.
(of the farmer)

☐ I practiced my flashcards today.

Latin Workbook - Level 3
Copyright © 1998 by Karen Mohs

LET'S PRACTICE

Write the meanings of these Latin sentences.

1. Fīlius fīliam amat, et fīlia fīlium.*

   It means The son likes the daughter, and the daughter likes the son.

2. Aquam spectō, sed nautās nōn vocō.

   It means I look at the water, but I do not call the sailors.

3. Nautae fēmina equōs lēgātī parat.

   It means The sailor's wife prepares the lieutenant's horses.

4. Fābulās poētārum et rēgīnārum nunc nārrāmus.

   It means Now we tell the stories of the poets and of the queens.

5. Lēgātus gladium dat, sed causam nōn dat.

   It means The envoy gives the sword, but he does not give the reason.

6. Amīcus fīliārum nāvigat, et epistulās exspectat.

   It means The friend of the daughters sails, and he awaits the letters.

7. Gladiōs socī occupō, et populōs pugnō.

   It means I seize the comrade's swords, and I fight the tribes.

8. Nūntiōs convocāmus, et fāmās laudāmus.

   It means We assemble the messengers, and we praise the reports.

9. Agricola fēminam et poētam et servum vocat.

   It means The farmer calls the woman and the poet and the slave.

*It appears that this second clause is without a verb. However, the verb amat, which is seen in the first clause, is understood to be the verb of the second clause as well.

☐ I practiced my flashcards today.

LET'S PRACTICE

Circle the correct Latin words.

of fortunes	he dwells	of the school
fortūnās **(fortūnārum)** fortūnae	**(habitat)** habitāmus habitō	lūdōrum lūdōs **(lūdī)**
native lands	of the lives	we please
(patriās) patria patriārum	vītās **(vītārum)** vītae	**(dēlectāmus)** dēlectat dēlectō
of the lands	I sail	care
terrae **(terrārum)** terrās	nāvigāmus nāvigat **(nāvigō)**	dīligentiae dīligentiās **(dīligentiam)**
friendliness	of the tongues	natures
(amīcitiam) amīcitiās amīcitiārum	linguae **(linguārum)** lingua	nātūrārum nātūram **(nātūrās)**
of the year	I dwell	of the memories
annōrum **(annī)** annus	habitat habitāmus **(habitō)**	**(memoriārum)** memoriam memoriās

I practiced my flashcards today.

78

Puellam amō.   It means **I like the girl.**

Puellam amāmus.   It means **We like the girl.**

Puellam amat.   It means **He (she, it) likes the girl.**

Puellam amant.   It means *They* **like the girl.**

Fill in the blank with ō or āmus or at or ant.

If I want to say *he* does something, I use the ending ___at___.

If I want to say *I* do something, I use the ending ___ō___.

If I want to say *they* do something, I use the ending ___ant___.

If I want to say *we* do something, I use the ending ___āmus___.

Write the meanings on the lines below the Latin sentences.

Amīcōs exspectat.	Tubam spectō.
He awaits the friends.	_I look at the trumpet._
Amīcum exspectant.	Tubās spectant.
They await the friend.	_They look at the trumpets._
Rēgīnās laudant.	Īnsulam occupāmus.
They praise the queens.	_We capture the island._
Rēgīnam laudāmus.	Īnsulās occupat.
We praise the queen.	_He captures the islands._

☐ I practiced my flashcards today. (Add the new cards.)

LET'S PRACTICE

Match the words to their meanings.

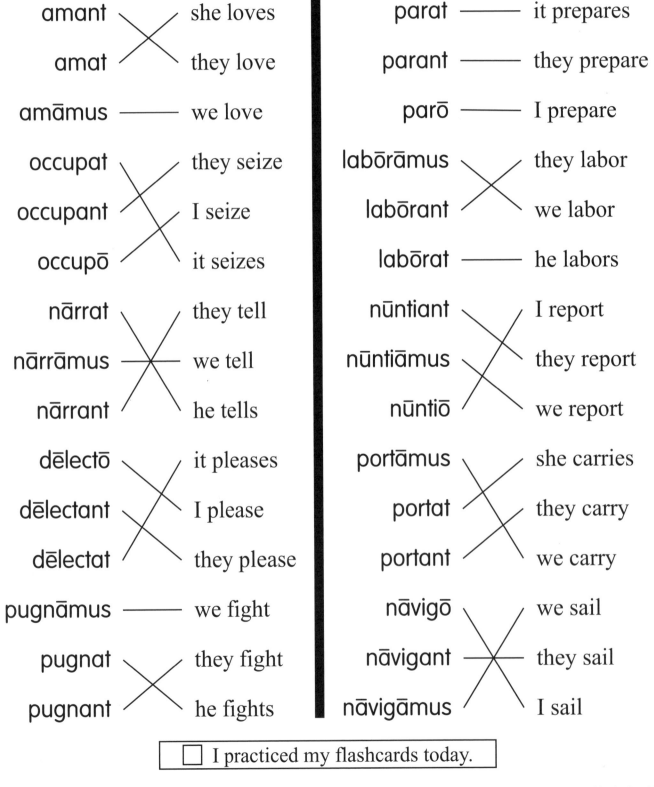

amant — she loves
amat — they love
amāmus — we love

occupat — they seize
occupant — I seize
occupō — it seizes

nārrat — they tell
nārrāmus — we tell
nārrant — he tells

dēlectō — it pleases
dēlectant — I please
dēlectat — they please

pugnāmus — we fight
pugnat — they fight
pugnant — he fights

parat — it prepares
parant — they prepare
parō — I prepare

labōrāmus — they labor
labōrant — we labor
labōrat — he labors

nūntiant — I report
nūntiāmus — they report
nūntiō — we report

portāmus — she carries
portat — they carry
portant — we carry

nāvigō — we sail
nāvigant — they sail
nāvigāmus — I sail

☐ I practiced my flashcards today.

LET'S PRACTICE

Write the sentences using the words on the right.

1. Fīliōs convocant.

It means **They summon the sons.**

| convocant |
| epistulam |
| fīliōs |
| fīlius |
| nāvigat |
| portō |

2. Fīlius nāvigat.

It means **The son sails.**

3. Epistulam portō.

It means **I carry the letter.**

4. Campōs spectāmus.

It means **We look at the plains.**

| campōs |
| poētam |
| poētās |
| spectāmus |
| spectō |
| vocant |

5. Poētās vocant.

It means **They call the poets.**

6. Poētam spectō.

It means **I look at the poet.**

☐ I practiced my flashcards today.

LET'S PRACTICE

Connect each orange to the correct basket.

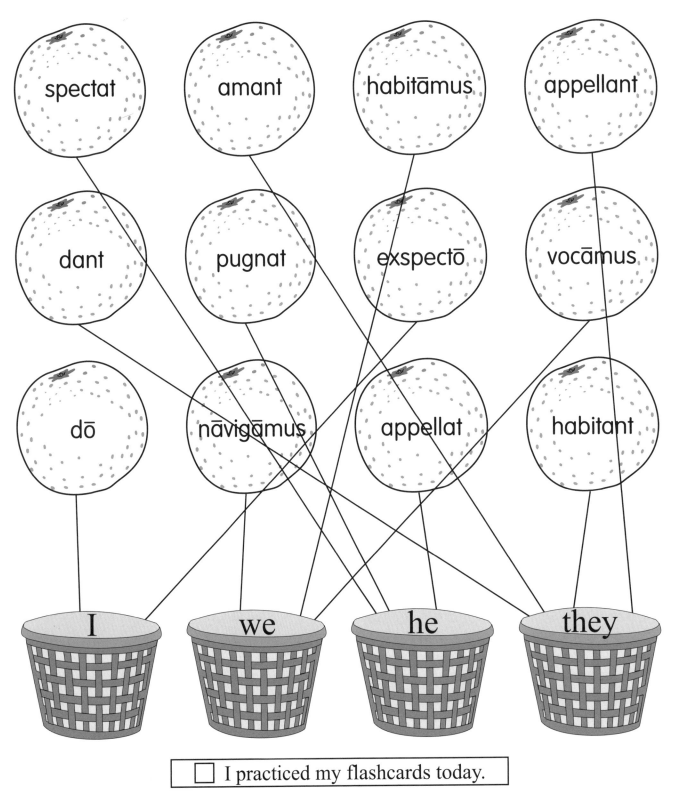

I practiced my flashcards today.

Now for more than one!

puella	It means **the girl.**
puellae*	It means **the *girls*.**
fēmina	It means **the woman.**
fēminae	It means **the *women*.**

filius	It means **the son.**
filiī**	It means **the *sons*.**
equus	It means **the horse.**
equī	It means **the *horses*.**

It's your turn!

Fill in the blank with a or ae or ī or us.

Port__a__ means **the gate**.   Gladi__us__ means **the sword**.

Port__ae__ means **the gates**.   Gladi__ī__ means **the swords**.

*Sometimes endings for different uses have the same spelling. For example, puellae, as taught here, means more than one girl. However, as we have learned earlier, it can also mean that something belongs to the girl. (See page 39.)

**Notice that the words ending in ius retain the i of the base when meaning more than one, as in filiī. It will be remembered that, in singular words, the i was dropped when showing possession (i.e., when showing that something belongs to something, as in filī.) (See page 39.)

☐ I practiced my flashcards today. (Add the new cards.)

LET'S PRACTICE

Color the box orange if the English meaning matches the Latin word at the beginning of the row.

puellae	of the girls	girls	girl
campum	of the plain	plains	plain
amīcī	friends	friend	of the friends
vītās	life	of the lives	lives
poētae	of the poets	poet	poets
tubārum	trumpets	of the trumpets	of the trumpet
patriae	of the country	of the countries	country
viae	street	streets	of the streets
populī	tribes	of the tribes	tribe
fīlī	son	sons	of the son

☐ I practiced my flashcards today.

Latin Workbook - Level 3
Copyright © 1998 by Karen Mohs

LET'S PRACTICE

Match the words to their meanings.

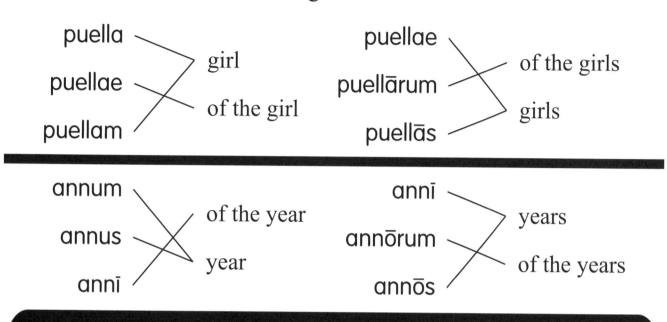

Put a check in the box when you notice:

☑ **Puella** and **puellam** both mean **girl**. The ending **a** is used to tell who is doing* the action. The ending **am** is used to tell who is receiving** the action.

☑ **Annus** and **annum** both mean **year**. The ending **us** is used to tell who is doing the action. The ending **um** is used to tell who is receiving the action.

☑ **Puellae** and **puellās** both mean **girls**. The ending **ae** is used to tell who is doing the action. The ending **ās** is used to tell who is receiving the action.

☑ **Annī** and **annōs** both mean **years**. The ending **ī** is used to tell who is doing the action. The ending **ōs** is used to tell who is receiving the action.

*This is the subject of the sentence.
**This is the object of the sentence.

☐ I practiced my flashcards today.

Puellam amant.

It means **They like the girl.**

Now let's use a word that tells us who *they* are.
Let's use *the farmers*.

Agricolae puellam amant.

It means **The farmers like the girl.**

Match the Latin sentences to their meanings.

_b_ 1. Fīliī laudant.

_a_ 2. Fīliōs laudant.

_c_ 3. Fīliae dēlectant.

_d_ 4. Fīliās dēlectant.

_e_ 5. Fēminae convocant.

_f_ 6. Fēminās convocant.

_h_ 7. Nūntiī pugnant.

_g_ 8. Nūntiōs pugnant.

a. They praise the sons.

b. The sons praise.

c. The daughters please.

d. They please the daughters.

e. The wives summon.

f. They summon the wives.

g. They fight the messengers.

h. The messengers fight.

☐ I practiced my flashcards today.

LET'S PRACTICE

Choose the best words for the sentences below. Then write what the sentences mean.

poēta	litterās	sociōrum

1. **Litterās** _____ et tubās portant.

It means _They carry the epistle and the trumpets._

2. Agricolae fāmās **sociōrum** _____ exspectant.

It means _The farmers await the reports of the allies._

3. **Poēta** _____ filiās fēminārum nōn dēlectat.

It means _The poet does not please the daughters of the women._

servōrum	servī	servōs

1. Puella **servōs** _____ populōrum convocat.

It means _The girl summons the slaves of the nations._

2. **Servī** _____ appellant viās patriārum.

It means _The slaves name the roads of the native lands._

3. Nautae equōs **servōrum** _____ vocant.

It means _The sailors call the slaves' horses._

☐ I practiced my flashcards today.

LET'S PRACTICE

Connect each lightning bolt to the correct cloud.

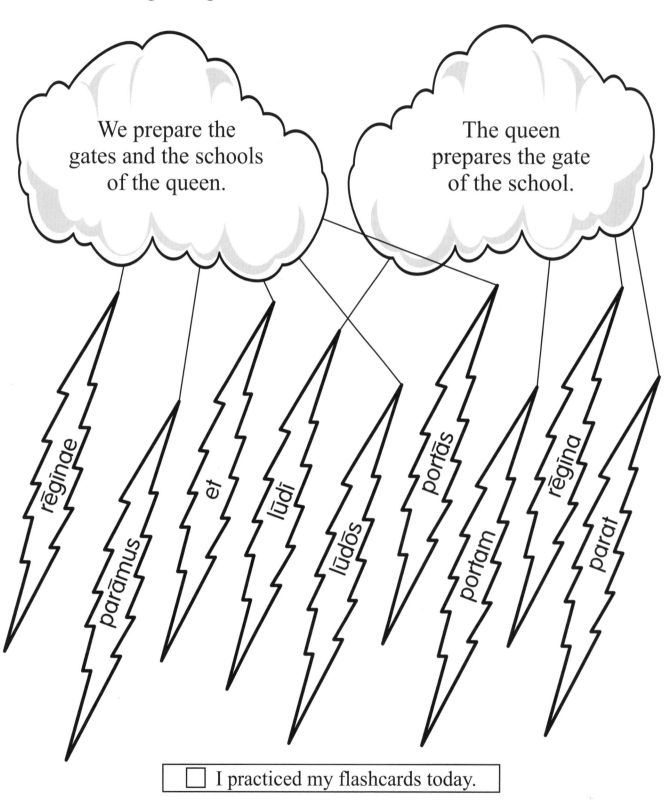

We prepare the gates and the schools of the queen.

The queen prepares the gate of the school.

rēgīnae

parāmus

et

lūdī

lūdōs

portās

portam

rēgīna

parat

☐ I practiced my flashcards today.

LET'S PRACTICE

Fill in the blanks with the correct Latin words. Then write what the sentences mean.

1. Lēgātī aquās īnsulae **spectant**.
   (look at)

   It means _The lieutenants look at the waters of the island._

2. Pugnāmus populum **amīcī** agricolae.
   (of the friend)

   It means _We fight the people of the farmer's friend._

3. **Sociī** fābulam nautārum nūntiant.
   (the comrades)

   It means _The comrades report the sailors' story._

4. Rēgīnae parant terram, sed nōn **labōrant**.
   (suffer)

   It means _The queens prepare the land, but they do not suffer._

5. Silvās et īnsulās **terrae** laudō.
   (of the earth)

   It means _I praise the forests and the islands of the earth._

☐ I practiced my flashcards today.

PUZZLE TIME

Think of the meanings of the English words. Then write the Latin words on the puzzle below.

across
1. I await
3. I announce
7. boy
8. play
10. now
12. I assemble
13. rumor
14. reason
16. slave
17. near
18. I give
19. queen

down
2. but
3. I tell
4. news
5. earth
6. memory
8. envoy
9. comrade
11. story
14. with
15. I like

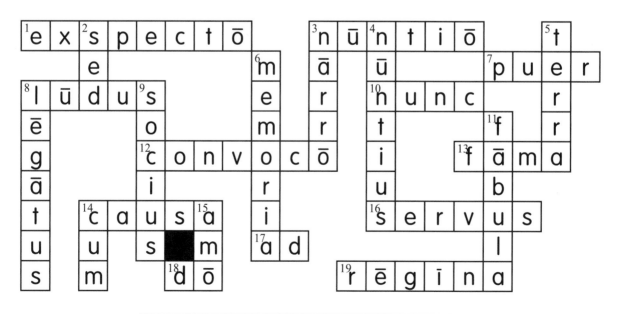

☐ I practiced my flashcards today.

Latin Workbook - Level 3
Copyright © 1998 by Karen Mohs

LET'S PRACTICE

Draw lines to connect the parts of the sentences.

1. Sociī equum rēgīnae   patriam nūntī.

2. Puella lēgātōs et agricolās   laudant.

3. Nunc nōn amō   convocat.

Now write the sentences you have made. First write them in Latin. Then write what they mean.

1. Sociī equum rēgīnae laudant.

It means _The comrades praise the queen's horse._

2. Puella lēgātōs et agricolās convocat.

It means _The girl assembles the lieutenants and the farmers._

3. Nunc nōn amō patriam nūntī.

It means _Now I do not love the messenger's native land._

CHALLENGE!
Can you write this sentence in Latin?

The son of the woman carries the sword of the sailor.

Fīlius fēminae gladium nautae portat.

☐ I practiced my flashcards today.

LET'S PRACTICE

Draw pictures for these sentences.

Fēminae agricolās exspectant, sed agricolae fēminās nōn exspectant.

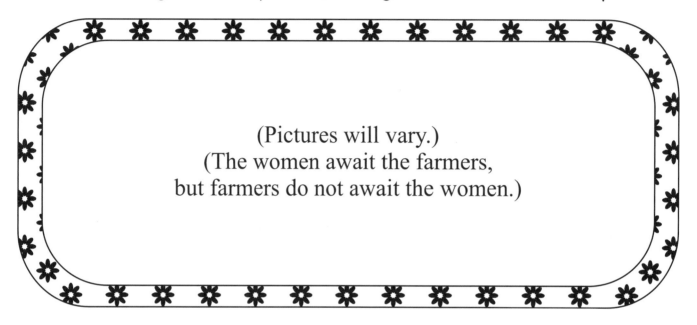

(Pictures will vary.)
(The women await the farmers,
but farmers do not await the women.)

Īnsulam nunc occupāmus, et litterās portāmus.

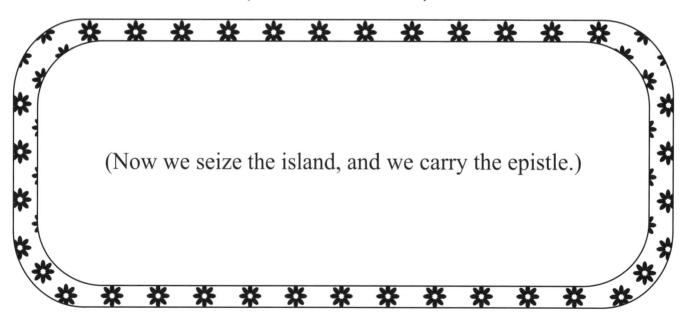

(Now we seize the island, and we carry the epistle.)

☐ I practiced my flashcards today.

superō

means

**I surpass,
I defeat**

Write the Latin word that means **I defeat**.

superō

superō

superō

Write the Latin word that means **plenty**.

cōpia

cōpia

cōpia

cōpia

means

**plenty,
supply**

in

means

**into, against,
in, on**

Write the Latin word that means **in**.

in

in

in

☐ I practiced my flashcards today. (Add the new cards.)

LET'S PRACTICE

Circle the correct Latin words.

on	I defeat	we are hard pressed
ad cum (in)	superat (superō) superāmus	(labōrāmus) labōrat labōrant
lives	I call	they grant
vītārum (vītās) vīta	(vocō) vocāmus vocant	dat dō (dant)
reason	we dwell	of care
causae causārum (causam)	habitō habitat (habitāmus)	(dīligentiae) dīligentia dīligentiam
she tells	plenty	friendships
nārrant nārrāmus (nārrat)	(cōpia) cōpiae cōpiārum	(amīcitiae) amīcitia amīcitiārum
he sails	of fortunes	they prepare
(nāvigat) nāvigāmus nāvigant	fortūnās (fortūnārum) fortūnam	parāmus parat (parant)

☐ I practiced my flashcards today.

94

oppugnō

means

I attack

Write the Latin word that means **I attack**.

oppugnō

oppugnō

oppugnō

Write the Latin word that means **long**.

diū

diū

diū

diū

means

for a long time, long

vulnerō

means

I wound

Write the Latin word that means **I wound**.

vulnerō

vulnerō

vulnerō

☐ I practiced my flashcards today. (Add the new cards.)

LET'S PRACTICE

Write the meanings of these Latin words.

Latin	Meaning		Latin	Meaning
agricolās	farmers		portant	they carry
vocāmus	we call		vīta	life
laudant	they praise		annōs	years
nāvigō	I sail		fābulās	stories
servus	slave		gladī	of the sword
nātūra	nature		annum	year
fīliam	daughter		sociī	comrades, allies
diū	for a long time, long		poēta	poet
fīliī	sons		oppugnō	I attack
porta	gate		dēlectat	he pleases
īnsulās	islands		amīcum	friend
vulnerat	he wounds		vītārum	of the lives
annōrum	of the years		pugnant	they fight
silvam	forest		rēgina	queen
fīlī	of the son		vocō	I call

☐ I practiced my flashcards today.

Latin Workbook - Level 3
Copyright © 1998 by Karen Mohs

fuga

means

flight, exile

Write the Latin word that means **flight**.

fuga

fuga

fuga

Write the Latin word that means **already**.

iam

iam

iam

iam

means

now, already

temptō

means

I try, I attempt

Write the Latin word that means **I try**.

temptō

temptō

temptō

☐ I practiced my flashcards today. (Add the new cards.)

LET'S PRACTICE

Match the words to their meanings.

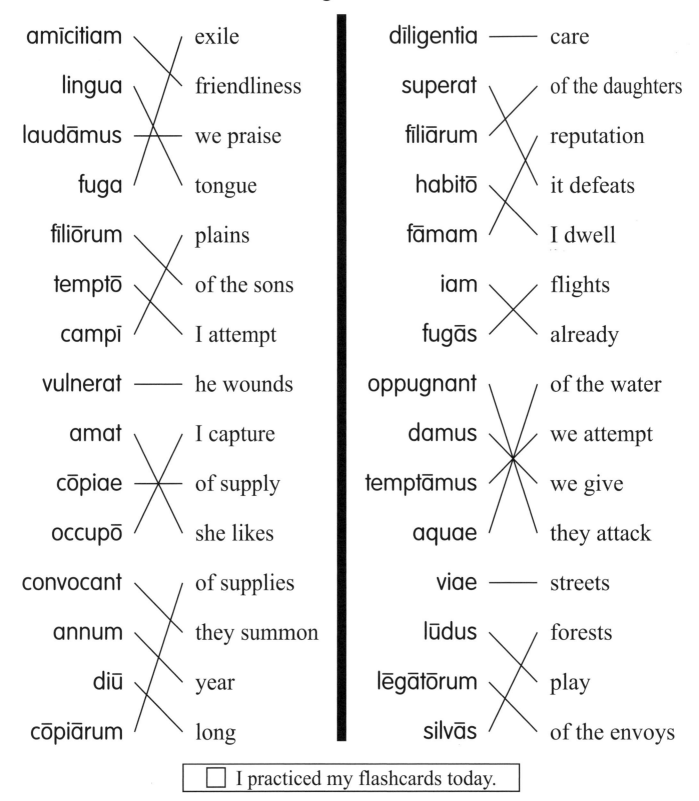

amīcitiam — exile
lingua — friendliness
laudāmus — we praise
fuga — tongue

filiōrum — plains
temptō — of the sons
campī — I attempt

vulnerat — he wounds

amat — I capture
cōpiae — of supply
occupō — she likes

convocant — of supplies
annum — they summon
diū — year
cōpiārum — long

dīligentia — care
superat — of the daughters
filiārum — reputation
habitō — it defeats
fāmam — I dwell

iam — flights
fugās — already

oppugnant — of the water
damus — we attempt
temptāmus — we give
aquae — they attack

viae — streets
lūdus — forests
lēgātōrum — play
silvās — of the envoys

☐ I practiced my flashcards today.

98

Latin Workbook - Level 3
Copyright © 1998 by Karen Mohs

herī

herī

means

yesterday

Write the Latin word that means **yesterday**.

herī

herī

herī

Write the Latin word that means **I keep**.

servō

servō

servō

servō

servō

means

I guard, I save, I keep

poena

poena

means

penalty, punishment

Write the Latin word that means **penalty**.

poena

poena

poena

☐ I practiced my flashcards today. (Add the new cards.)

LET'S PRACTICE

Color the box red if the English meaning matches the Latin word at the beginning of the row.

amīcī	of the friends	of the friend	friend
herī	today	tomorrow	yesterday
vulnerant	we wound	they wound	it wounds
fugae	flights	of the flights	flight
servat	they guard	she guards	I guard
iam	already	where	today
cōpiam	supply	of the supplies	supplies
causās	cause	causes	of the causes
poena	of the penalty	penalties	penalty
epistula	letter	of the letter	of the letters

☐ I practiced my flashcards today.

Write the Latin word that means **always**.

semper

means

always

semper

semper

semper

Write the Latin word that means **captive**.

captīvus

captīvus

captīvus

captīvus

means

captive

Write the Latin word that means **place**.

locus

means

place, location, situation

locus

locus

locus

☐ I practiced my flashcards today. (Add the new cards.)

LET'S PRACTICE

Choose the correct words for the sentences. Put them in the blanks.
Then write what the sentences mean.

Fīliī - Fīlī

1. **Fīliī** superant agricolās rēgīnae.

It means _The sons defeat the queen's farmers._

nūntiī - nūntiōs

2. Semper oppugnō **nūntiōs**.

It means _I always attack the messengers._

spectant - spectat

3. Captīvī **spectant** servum.

It means _The captives look at the slave._

Poenae - Poenam

4. **Poenam** populī nūntiāmus.

It means _We report the punishment of the people._

vulnerat - vulnerant

5. Equus puellās **vulnerat**.

It means _The horse wounds the girls._

īnsula - īnsulae

6. Portam **īnsulae** servāmus.

It means _We guard the island's gate._

oppugnō - oppugnat

7. Populus nōn **oppugnat**.

It means _The people do not attack._

☐ I practiced my flashcards today.

audācia

means

boldness, daring

Write the Latin word that means **daring**.

audācia

audācia

audācia

Write the Latin word that means **today**.

hodiē

hodiē

hodiē

hodiē

means

today

volō

means

I fly

Write the Latin word that means **I fly**.

volō

volō

volō

☐ I practiced my flashcards today. (Add the new cards.)

LET'S PRACTICE

Write the Latin words.

they announce	nūntiant	it tries	temptat
of the penalty	poenae	I dwell	habitō
she prepares	parat	yesterday	herī
I fly	volō	of the native lands	patriārum
we give	damus	we surpass	superāmus
already	iam	they attempt	temptant
we save	servāmus	he likes	amat
of the flight	fugae	I attack	oppugnō
he fights	pugnat	today	hodiē
I name	appellō	they wound	vulnerant
always	semper	of the year	annī
they sail	nāvigant	of the poet	poētae

☐ I practiced my flashcards today.

Latin Workbook - Level 3
Copyright © 1998 by Karen Mohs

animus

means

mind, spirit

Write the Latin word that means **mind**.

animus

animus

animus

Write the Latin word that means **tomorrow**.

crās

crās

crās

crās

means

tomorrow

carrus

means

cart, wagon

Write the Latin word that means **cart**.

carrus

carrus

carrus

☐ I practiced my flashcards today. (Add the new cards.)

LET'S PRACTICE

Color the box purple if the Latin word matches the English meaning at the beginning of the row.

punishment	poenās	poena	poenārum
daring	audāciae	audāciam	audāciās
of the captive	captīvī	captīvōrum	captīvōs
tomorrow	herī	hodiē	crās
exiles	fuga	fugam	fugās
wagon	carrī	carrus	carrōrum
situations	locus	locī	locōrum
of the daughters	filiārum	filiās	filia
care	dīligentiās	dīligentiae	dīligentia
mind	animus	animōs	animōrum

☐ I practiced my flashcards today.

LET'S PRACTICE

Write the meanings of these Latin words.

dēlectō	I please		diū	for a long time, long
servōrum	of the slaves		sociī	comrades, allies
temptō	I attempt		occupat	he seizes, he captures
carrōs	carts, wagons		audācia	boldness, daring
volāmus	we fly		iam	now, already
epistula	letter, epistle		animum	mind, spirit
semper	always		filiōrum	of the sons
cōpia	plenty, supply		porta	gate
vīta	life		servāmus	we guard, we save, we keep
captīvōs	captives		lēgātus	lieutenant, envoy
nāvigat	he sails		nārrant	they relate, they tell
lūdum	game, play, school		nātūra	nature
lingua	tongue, language		causās	causes, reasons
oppugnant	they attack		via	road, way, street
gladiī	swords		vulnerō	I wound

☐ I practiced my flashcards today.

LET'S PRACTICE

Color the hat yellow if the words mean the same.

they love / amant	penalties / poenās	he keeps / servō	yesterday / herī
I defeat / superant	of the ally / socī	place / locum	they fly / volō
flights / fugae	she carries / portāmus	friends / audāciās	I call / vocō
of the wagons / carrum	today / hodiē	I report / nūntiō	plenty / cōpiam

☐ I practiced my flashcards today.

LET'S PRACTICE

Match the words to their meanings.

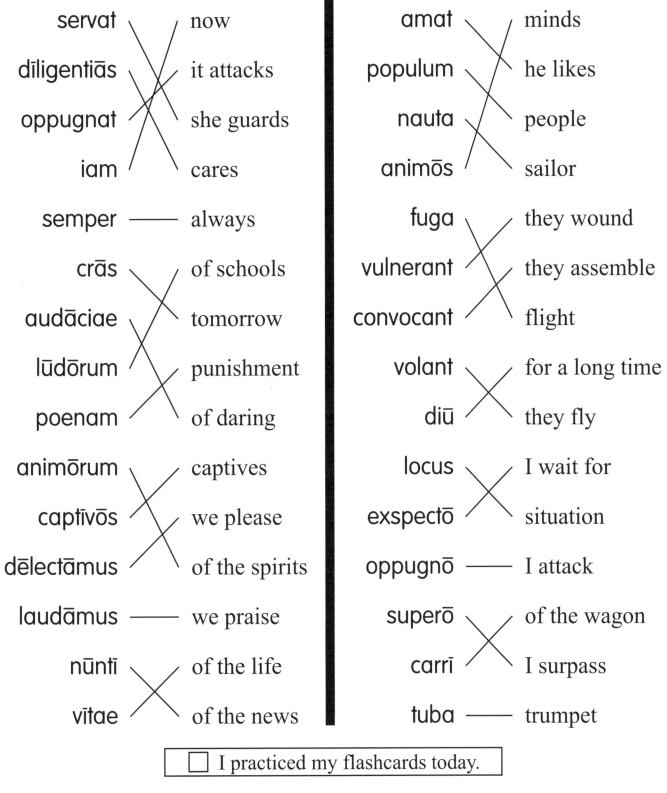

servat — now
dīligentiās — it attacks
oppugnat — she guards
iam — cares

semper —— always

crās — of schools
audāciae — tomorrow
lūdōrum — punishment
poenam — of daring

animōrum — captives
captivōs — we please
dēlectāmus — of the spirits

laudāmus —— we praise

nūntī — of the life
vītae — of the news

amat — minds
populum — he likes
nauta — people
animōs — sailor

fuga — they wound
vulnerant — they assemble
convocant — flight

volant — for a long time
diū — they fly

locus — I wait for
exspectō — situation

oppugnō —— I attack

superō — of the wagon
carrī — I surpass

tuba —— trumpet

☐ I practiced my flashcards today.

LET'S PRACTICE

Shoot the arrows to their targets.

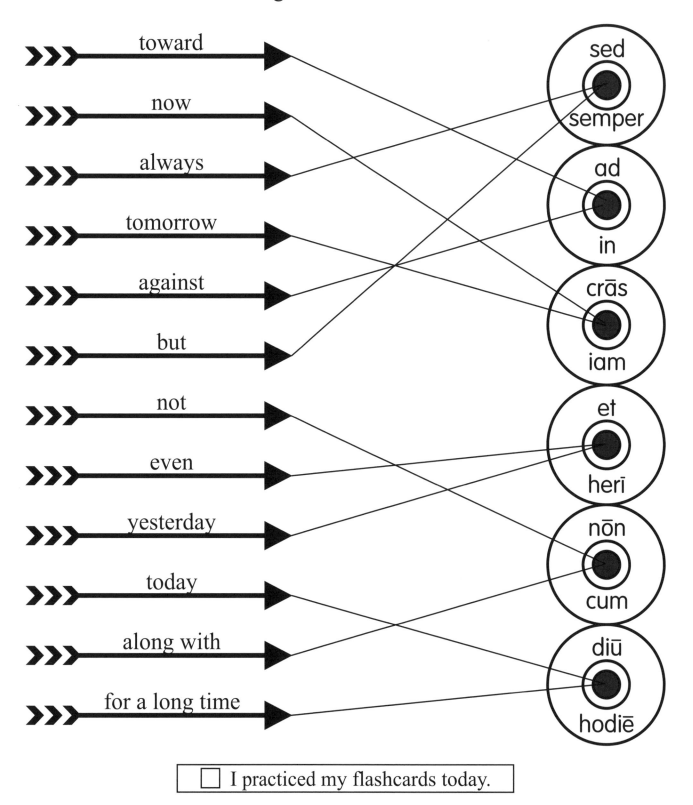

toward
now
always
tomorrow
against
but
not
even
yesterday
today
along with
for a long time

sed
semper
ad
in
crās
iam
et
herī
nōn
cum
diū
hodiē

☐ I practiced my flashcards today.

110

LET'S PRACTICE

Put the endings in the boxes on the Latin words in the sentences.

| am at | 1. Puell<u>a</u> fēmin<u>am</u> naut<u>ae</u> port<u>at</u>. |
| ae a | It means **The girl carries the sailor's wife.** |

| ōrum ās | 2. Anim<u>ōs</u> soci<u>ōrum</u> nunc laud<u>āmus</u>. |
| āmus ōs | It means **Now we praise the minds of the allies.** |

| ant ae | 3. Poēt<u>ae</u> memori<u>ās</u> popul<u>ōrum</u> serv<u>ant</u>. |
| ās ōrum | It means **The poets keep the nations' memories.** |

| at ō | 4. Gladi<u>um</u> port<u>ō</u>, sed nōn pugn<u>ō</u>. |
| ō um | It means **I carry the sword, but I do not fight.** |

| at ōs | 5. Vulner<u>at</u> et super<u>at</u> lēgāt<u>ōs</u> rēgīn<u>ae</u>. |
| ae at | It means **He wounds and defeats the queen's envoys.** |

| at us | 6. Captīv<u>us</u> carr<u>ōs</u> īnsul<u>ae</u> laud<u>at</u>. |
| ōs ae | It means **The captive praises the island's carts.** |

☐ I practiced my flashcards today.

Connect each bowling pin to the correct bowling ball.

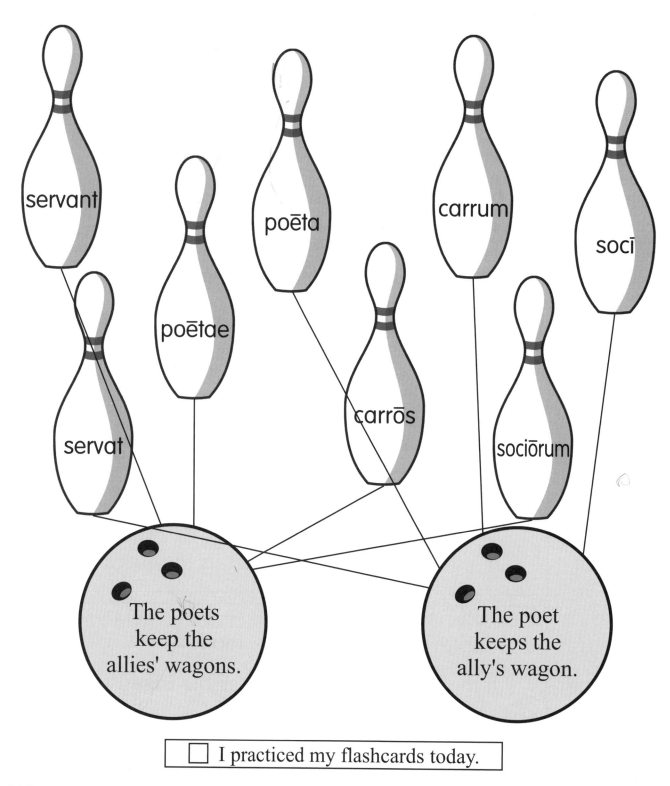

servant

poēta

carrum

socī

poētae

servat

carrōs

sociōrum

The poets keep the allies' wagons.

The poet keeps the ally's wagon.

☐ I practiced my flashcards today.

LET'S PRACTICE

Circle the correct Latin words. Then write what the sentences mean.

1. Nūntius hodiē (portat) / portant cōpiās amīcōrum.

   It means Today the messenger carries the friends' supplies.

2. Dīligentiam filiārum rēgīna nunc exspectāmus. / (exspectat.)

   It means Now the queen awaits the diligence of the daughters.

3. Fīliōs lēgātī vocāmus, sed nōn fīlia. / (filiās.)

   It means We call the envoy's sons, but we do not call the daughters.

4. (Prōvinciās) / Prōvinciae oppugnō, sed populōs nōn superō.

   It means I attack the provinces, but I do not defeat the tribes.

5. Sociī equōs et gladius / (gladiōs) iam parant.

   It means The comrades already prepare the horses and the swords.

6. Puella vīllam et silvam et īnsulam dant. / (dat.)

   It means The girl gives the villa and the forest and the island.

7. Poenās nūntiāmus (nautārum) / nauta et agricolārum.

   It means We report the punishments of the sailors and farmers.

8. Fēmina fīliam et fīlium amīcī convocāmus. / (convocat.)

   It means The woman assembles the friend's daughter and son.

9. Fīlius / (Fīliī) locōs et portās lūdōrum spectant.

   It means The sons look at the schools' locations and gates.

☐ I practiced my flashcards today.

LET'S PRACTICE

Draw pictures for these sentences.

Equī hodiē volant, sed tubae et carrī nōn volant.

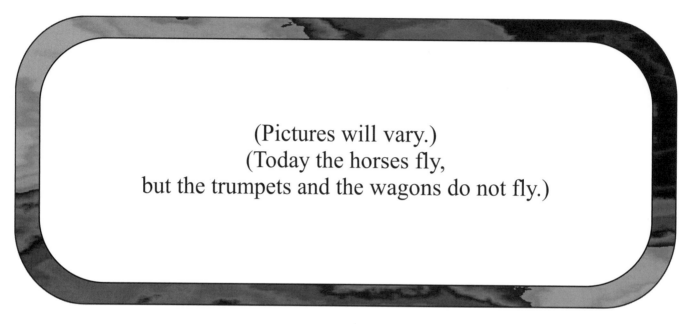

(Pictures will vary.)
(Today the horses fly,
but the trumpets and the wagons do not fly.)

Nauta fābulās īnsulae et patriae diū nārrat.

(For a long time, the sailor tells the stories
of the island and of the native land.)

☐ I practiced my flashcards today.

LET'S PRACTICE

Fill in the blanks with the correct words from the boxes on the right. Then write the meanings of the sentences.

1. Nautae __agricolās__ vulnerant.

   It means The sailors wounded the farmers.

puella agricola agricolās

2. Poētam laudāmus __populī__.

   It means We praise the poet of the people.

pugnō populī nūntiī

3. __Habitat__, et rēgīnam dēlectat.

   It means He lives, and he pleases the queen.

Habitat Campōrum Fīliī

4. Epistulās fīlī diū __spectō__.

   It means I look at the son's letters for a long time.

crās herī spectō

5. __Causās__ fugae nunc nārrāmus.

   It means We now tell the causes of the exile.

Causās Fābula Habitō

6. Amīcōs __fēminārum__ semper vocant.

   It means They always call the wives' friends.

fēminōs fēminārum fēmina

7. Fāmās prōvinciārum hodiē __damus__.

   It means Today we give the reports of the provinces.

audāciae cum damus

☐ I practiced my flashcards today.

PUZZLE TIME

Think of the meanings of the English words. Then write the Latin words on the puzzle below.

across
1. boldness
8. penalty
9. yesterday
10. story
12. where?
13. captive
16. always
17. I please
19. I guard
21. I fly
22. rumor

down	
1. mind	17. I grant
2. wagon	18. with
3. toward	20. and
4. way	
5. situation	
6. already	
7. flight	
9. today	
11. I try	
13. tomorrow	
14. boy	
15. I like	

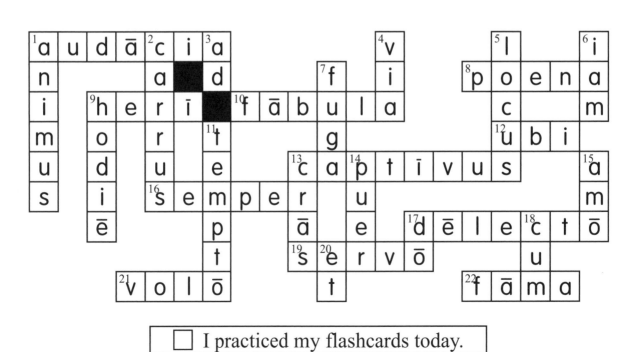

☐ I practiced my flashcards today.

116

Amō puellam.   It means **I like the girl.**

Amās puellam.   It means **You like the girl.**

(The ending ās means only one *you*. When there are several of *you*, a different word is used. We will learn it later.)

Portō gladium.   It means **I carry the sword.**

Portās gladium.   It means **You carry the sword.**

Match the Latin words to their meanings.

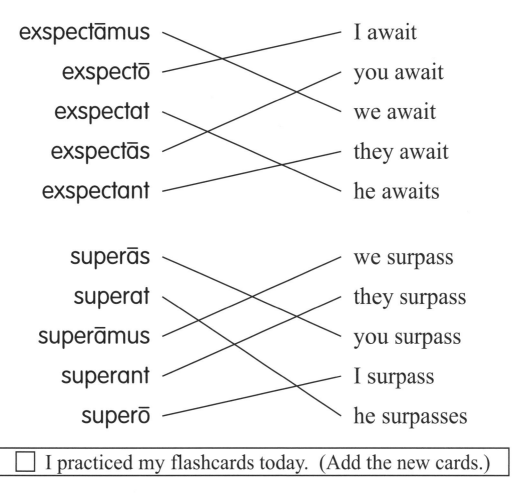

exspectāmus   I await

exspectō   you await

exspectat   we await

exspectās   they await

exspectant   he awaits

superās   we surpass

superat   they surpass

superāmus   you surpass

superant   I surpass

superō   he surpasses

☐ I practiced my flashcards today. (Add the new cards.)

LET'S PRACTICE

Fill in the blanks with the correct Latin words. Then write what the sentences mean.

1. Vīllās fēminārum poētārum _____ **amās** _____.
   (you love)

   It means _You love the farmhouses of the poets' wives._

2. Agricolae tubās _____ **puellārum** _____ hodiē occupant.
   (of the girls)

   It means _The farmers seize the girls' trumpets today._

3. Locum portae vīllae diū _____ **spectās** _____.
   (you look at)

   It means _You look at the location of the villa's gate for a long time._

4. Captīvus lēgātum et sociōs _____ **pugnat** _____.
   (fights)

   It means _The captive fights the lieutenant and the allies._

5. Animum et _____ **audāciam** _____ agricolae laudās.
   (the boldness)

   It means _You praise the spirit and the boldness of the farmer._

   ☐ I practiced my flashcards today.

Latin Workbook - Level 3
Copyright © 1998 by Karen Mohs

LET'S PRACTICE

Write the meanings of these Latin sentences.

1. Agricola animōs servōrum iam parat.

   It means <u>The farmer already prepares the minds of the slaves.</u>

2. Amīcum puellae pugnās, sed nōn socium.

   It means <u>You fight the girl's friend, but you do not fight the comrade.</u>

3. Epistulās portāmus, et captīvōs appellāmus.

   It means <u>We carry the letters, and we address the captives.</u>

4. Nōn semper das causam fugae equōrum.

   It means <u>You do not always give the cause of the horses' flight.</u>

5. Nūntiō poenam populōrum et rēgīnārum.

   It means <u>I report the punishment of the tribes and of the queens.</u>

6. Servōs servās, sed amīcōs nōn amās.

   It means <u>You guard the slaves, but you do not love the friends.</u>

7. Equus portam spectat, et agricolam oppugnat.

   It means <u>The horse looks at the gate, and he attacks the farmer.</u>

8. Fābulam semper nārrās memoriārum nūntiōrum.

   It means <u>You always tell the story of the messengers' memories.</u>

9. Puellae annōs cōpiae diū exspectant.

   It means <u>The girls wait a long time for the years of plenty.</u>

10. Amīcitiam prōvinciārum filī nōn superās.

    It means <u>You do not surpass the friendliness of the son's provinces.</u>

☐ I practiced my flashcards today.

LET'S PRACTICE

Connect each key to the correct key ring.

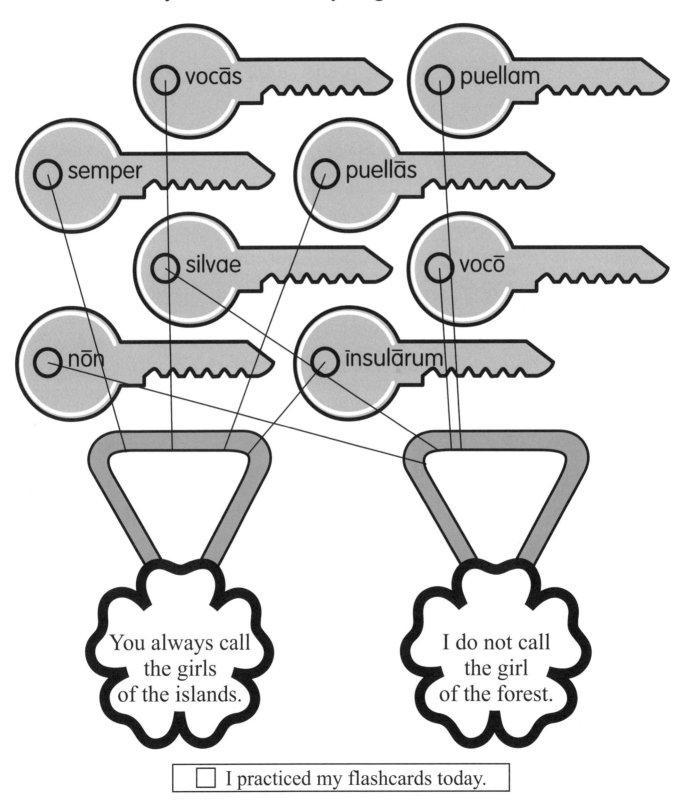

vocās

puellam

semper

puellās

silvae

vocō

nōn

īnsulārum

You always call
the girls
of the islands.

I do not call
the girl
of the forest.

☐ I practiced my flashcards today.

Puella habitat.　　It means **The girl lives.**

Now let's tell *where* the girl lives.

In īnsulā puella habitat.

It means **The girl lives on the island.**

In lūdō puella habitat.

It means **The girl lives in the school.**

Now read these Latin sentences.　Write what they mean.

1. In silvā habitāmus.

   It means　We live in the forest.

2. In campō pugnās.

   It means　You fight on the plain.

Put a check in the box when you notice:

☑ The Latin word in can mean *in* or *on*.

☑ The new ending ā is used with words ending in a like the word īnsula.

☑ The new ending ō is used with words ending in us like the word lūdus.

☐ I practiced my flashcards today.　(Add the new cards.)

LET'S PRACTICE

Match the Latin sentences to their meanings.

__d__ 1. Fābulam in vīllā nārrō.   a. You tell the story in the villa.

__a__ 2. Fābulam in vīllā nārrās.   b. She tells the stories in the villa.

__e__ 3. Fābulās in vīllā nārrās.   c. We tell the stories in the villa.

__b__ 4. Fābulās in vīllā nārrat.   d. I tell the story in the villa.

__c__ 5. Fābulās in vīllā nārrāmus.   e. You tell the stories in the villa.

__h__ 6. Exspectō filiōs in īnsulā.   f. He awaits the sons on the island.

__f__ 7. In īnsulā filiōs exspectat.   g. You await the son on the island.

__j__ 8. Exspectat filiōs īnsula.   h. I await the sons on the island.

__i__ 9. Fīliī exspectant īnsulam.   i. The sons await the island.

__g__ 10. In īnsulā exspectās filium.   j. The island awaits the sons.

__o__ 11. Sociōs in aquā vulnerō.   k. I wound the ally in the water.

__k__ 12. In aquā socium vulnerō.   l. The water wounds the ally.

__m__ 13. Sociōs in aquā vulnerat.   m. It wounds the allies in the water.

__l__ 14. Vulnerat socium aqua.   n. The waters wound the allies.

__n__ 15. Sociōs aquae vulnerant.   o. I wound the allies in the water.

☐ I practiced my flashcards today.

In īnsulā puella habitat. It means **The girl lives on the island.**
In lūdō puella habitat. It means **The girl lives in the school.**

Now for more than one!

In īnsulīs puella habitat. It means **The girl lives on the *islands*.**
In lūdīs puella habitat. It means **The girl lives in the *schools*.**

Now read these Latin sentences. Write what they mean.

1. In vīllīs pugnat.

   It means _He fights in the farmhouses._

2. In equīs labōrās.

   It means _You labor on the horses._

Put a check in the box when you notice:

☑ The new plural ending **īs** is used with words ending in a like the word **īnsula**.

☑ The same plural ending **īs** is used with words ending in us like the word **lūdus**.

☐ I practiced my flashcards today. (Add the new cards.)

LET'S PRACTICE

Match the words to their meanings.

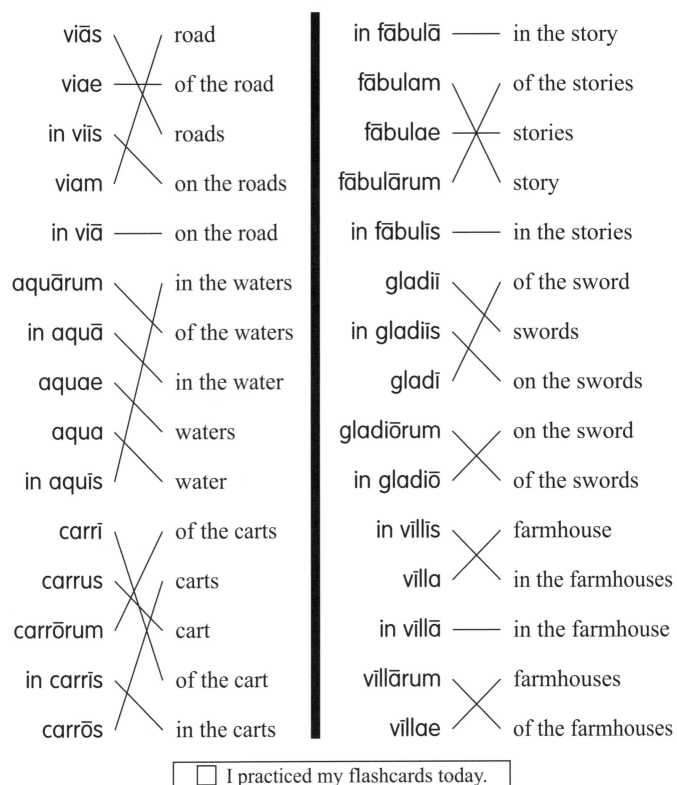

viās	road
viae	of the road
in viīs	roads
viam	on the roads
in viā	on the road
aquārum	in the waters
in aquā	of the waters
aquae	in the water
aqua	waters
in aquīs	water
carrī	of the carts
carrus	carts
carrōrum	cart
in carrīs	of the cart
carrōs	in the carts

in fābulā	in the story
fābulam	of the stories
fābulae	stories
fābulārum	story
in fābulīs	in the stories
gladiī	of the sword
in gladiīs	swords
gladī	on the swords
gladiōrum	on the sword
in gladiō	of the swords
in vīllīs	farmhouse
vīlla	in the farmhouses
in vīllā	in the farmhouse
vīllārum	farmhouses
vīllae	of the farmhouses

☐ I practiced my flashcards today.

124

Puellās convocō.   It means **I summon the girls.**

Now let's tell the *means* by which I summon the girls.

Puellās tubā convocō.

It means **I summon the girls on (by means of)* the trumpet.**

Puellās tubīs convocō.

It means **I summon the girls on (by means of)* the *trumpets*.**

Now read these Latin sentences. Write what they mean.

1. Lēgātōs gladiō pugnō.

   It means <u>I fight the lieutenants with a sword.</u>

2. Poētās laudant linguīs.

   It means <u>They praise the poets by means of the languages.</u>

Put a check in the box when you notice:

☑ It is the ending alone, without additional words, that tells the means by which something is done.

☑ The endings are the same as the endings used with the Latin word in (which is used to show *where* something is done).

*As the student translates, he may use any of a number of prepositions (***with***, ***in***, ***on***, etc.), but he must remember that the idea of this construction is "by means of."

☐ I practiced my flashcards today. (Add the new cards.)

LET'S PRACTICE

Circle the correct Latin words.

with swords	with the trumpet	on the wagon
in gladiīs gladiō (gladiīs)	in tubā (tubā) tubīs	(in carrō) carrōrum in carrīs
on the horse	**in the carts**	**in the provinces**
equōs (in equō) in equīs	(in carrīs) in carrō carrus	in prōvinciā prōvinciae (in prōvinciīs)
on the street	**with rumors**	**on the gate**
viae in viīs (in viā)	in fāmīs fāmā (fāmīs)	(in portā) in portīs portās
forests	**in the country houses**	**with the trumpets**
silvā in silvīs (silvae)	(in vīllīs) in vīllā vīllam	(tubīs) tubās tubā
in the schools	**farmhouses**	**on the horses**
(in lūdīs) in lūdō lūdus	in vīllā (vīllae) vīllārum	in equō equī (in equīs)

☐ I practiced my flashcards today.

Latin Workbook - Level 3
Copyright © 1998 by Karen Mohs

Pugnō.   It means **I fight.**

Now let's tell the *manner* in which I fight.

Cum audāciā pugnō.

It means **I fight with* boldness.**

Now read these Latin sentences. Write what they mean.

1. Cum dīligentiā labōrās.

   It means You labor with diligence.

2. Causam cum audāciā nūntiat.

   It means He announces the reason with boldness.

3. Vocō cum amīcitiā agricolās.

   It means I call the farmers with friendliness.

Put a check in the box when you notice:

☑ When expressing the manner in which something is done, we use the Latin word cum.

☑ The endings are the same as the endings used with the Latin word in (which is used to show *where* something is done).

*As the student translates, he may use the preposition *with*, but he must remember that the idea of this construction is the *manner* in which a thing is done.

☐ I practiced my flashcards today. (Add the new card.)

LET'S PRACTICE

Write the meanings on the lines below the Latin sentences.

Cum dīligentiā pugnat.	Gladiōs cum audāciā portō.
He fights with diligence.	I carry the swords with boldness.
Gladiīs pugnant.	Gladium in patriā portat.
They fight with swords.	He carries the sword in the country.
In vīllā habitat.	Nautās tubā convocāmus.
He lives in the farmhouse.	We assemble the sailors with the trumpet.
Cum amīcitiā habitat.	Nautae filiōs convocat.
He lives with friendliness.	He assembles the sailor's sons.

Write the correct Latin words on the lines beside the meanings.

on the island   **in īnsulā**

with friendliness   **cum amīcitiā**

in the forests   **in silvīs**

with the trumpet   **tubā**

with diligence   **cum dīligentiā**

with the swords   **gladiīs**

☐ I practiced my flashcards today.

128

Amās puellam.   It means **You like the girl.**

(when there is only one *you*)

Now for more than one *you*.

Amātis puellam.   It means **You like the girl.**

(when there are more than one *you*)

Color the block orange if the Latin word means only one *you*. Color it purple if the Latin word means more than one *you*.

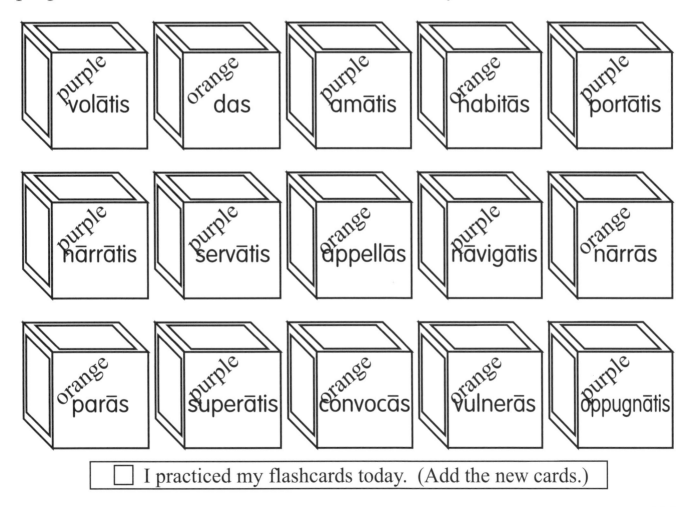

purple volātis   orange das   purple amātis   orange habitās   purple portātis

purple nārrātis   purple servātis   orange appellās   purple navigātis   orange nārrās

orange parās   purple superātis   orange convocās   orange vulnerās   purple oppugnātis

☐ I practiced my flashcards today. (Add the new cards.)

LET'S PRACTICE

Write the meanings of these Latin words.

amō <u>I love</u>   amāmus <u>we love</u>

amās <u>you (sing.) love</u>   amātis <u>you (pl.) love</u>

amat <u>he (she, it) loves</u>   amant <u>they love</u>

---

dō <u>I give</u>   damus <u>we give</u>

das <u>you (sing.) give</u>   datis <u>you (pl.) give</u>

dat <u>he (she, it) gives</u>   dant <u>they give</u>

---

volō <u>I fly</u>   volāmus <u>we fly</u>

volās <u>you (sing.) fly</u>   volātis <u>you (pl.) fly</u>

volat <u>he (she, it) flies</u>   volant <u>they fly</u>

---

nārrō <u>I tell</u>   nārrāmus <u>we tell</u>

nārrās <u>you (sing.) tell</u>   nārrātis <u>you (pl.) tell</u>

nārrat <u>he (she, it) tells</u>   nārrant <u>they tell</u>

☐ I practiced my flashcards today.

Latin Workbook - Level 3
Copyright © 1998 by Karen Mohs

LET'S PRACTICE

Put checks in the boxes of the correct Latin sentences.

The girls in the farmhouse always look at the horses on the plain.

- [ ] Puella in vīllā equōs in campīs semper spectat.
- [✔] Puellae in vīllā equōs in campō semper spectant.
- [ ] Puellās in vīllārum equōs in campō semper spectat.

The lieutenants do not attack the ally with diligence.

- [ ] Lēgātī socium nōn oppugnāmus cum dīligentiīs.
- [ ] Lēgātus sociōs nōn oppugnat cum dīligentiā.
- [✔] Lēgātī socium nōn oppugnant cum dīligentiā.

We live for a long time in the native land, and we love the villas.

- [✔] In patriā diū habitāmus, et vīllās amāmus.
- [ ] In patriīs diū habitant, et vīllīs amant.
- [ ] In patriā diū habitō, et vīllās amō.

The poet's son defeats the tribes in the forest, and he wounds the captives.

- [ ] Fīliī poēta populōs in silvā superant, et captīvōs vulnerat.
- [✔] Fīlius poētae populōs in silvā superat, et captīvōs vulnerat.
- [ ] Fīlius poētae populīs in silvīs superō, et captīvōs vulnerō.

You announce the news with boldness, but you do not love the country.

- [✔] Cum audāciā nūntium nūntiās, sed patriam nōn amās.
- [ ] In audāciā nūntium nūntiās, et patriās nōn amat.
- [ ] Cum audāciīs nūntium nūntiō, sed patriam nōn amāmus.

[ ] I practiced my flashcards today.

PUZZLE TIME

Find the hidden sentence. (Hint: It has three words.)

F	ē	m	l	a
ī	f	i	m	u
l	s	n	u	d
i	ā	ā	r	ō

Write the sentence.

Fīliās fēminārum laudō.

It means _I praise the women's daughters._

Match the Latin words to their meanings.

_d_ 1. nāvigant   a. you (plural) sail

_b_ 2. nāvigat   b. she sails

_e_ 3. nāvigāmus   c. you (singular) sail

_c_ 4. nāvigās   d. they sail

_a_ 5. nāvigātis   e. we sail

☐ I practiced my flashcards today.

Carrum dō.   It means **I give the cart.**

Now let's tell *to whom* I give the cart.

Puellae* carrum dō.   It means **I give the cart *to the girl.***
                                      or
                        I give the cart *for the girl.*

Fīliō** carrum dō.   It means **I give the cart *to the son.***
                                      or
                        I give the cart *for the son.*

Circle the correct Latin words. Then write what the sentences mean.

1. Puella
   (Puellae) aquam in carrō hodiē das.

   It means You give the water in the cart to the girl today.

2. Nūntiāmus (agricolae) in equō audāciam fīlī.
              agricola

   It means We announce to the farmer on the horse the son's boldness.

3. In silvā (lēgātō) tubam semper portō.
             legatus

   It means I always carry the trumpet for the envoy in the forest.

*Notice that the ending ae (on words like puella), in this case meaning *to* or *for* the girl, is identical to the ending of two other uses: the plural subject (the girls *doing* the action) and the singular possessive (*belonging to* the girl). (See pages 83 and 39.)

**Notice that the ending ō (on words like fīlius), in this case meaning *to* or *for* the son, is identical to the ending of another use: the place *where*. (See page 121.)

☐ I practiced my flashcards today. (Add the new cards.)

LET'S PRACTICE

Match the correct spelling of the Latin words to the sentences. Some answers may be used more than once.

_a_   1. The friend **of the girl** is here.

_a_   2. The mother gives **the girl** a bowl.

_b_   3. The friend **of the girls** is here.

_c_   4. The farmer looks at **the girls**.

_a_   5. **The girls** look at the farmer.

a. puellae
b. puellārum
c. puellās

_e_   6. The friend **of the son** has a horse.

_g_   7. The father hands **the son** a plow.

_f_   8. **The sons** like the boy.

_d_   9. The boy likes **the son**.

d. filium
e. filī
f. filiī
g. filiō

_i_ 10. She gave **the friend** a flower.

_j_ 11. The daughter **of the friend** is young.

_k_ 12. **The friend** smells the flowers.

_j_ 13. **The friends** smell the flowers.

_h_ 14. The girl has two **friends**.

h. amīcōs
i. amīcō
j. amīcī
k. amīcus

☐ I practiced my flashcards today.

Latin Workbook - Level 3
Copyright © 1998 by Karen Mohs

LET'S PRACTICE

Fill in the blanks with the correct Latin words. Then write what the sentences mean.

1. Puella __**rēgīnae**__ fāmās semper nūntiat.
(to the queen)

   It means _The girl always reports the rumors to the queen._

2. Damus hodiē agricolae carrōs et __**equōs**__.
(the horses)

   It means _We give the carts and the horses to the farmer today._

3. In aquīs īnsulae __**fīliī**__ fēminārum nāvigant.
(the sons)

   It means _The sons of the women sail in the island's waters._

4. Animī poētārum __**fīliō**__ fābulās nunc parant.
(for the son)

   It means _Now the poets' minds prepare the stories for the son._

5. Epistulam exspectātis, et amīcōs **servōrum** vocātis.
(of the slaves)

   It means _You await the letter, and you call the slaves' friends._

☐ I practiced my flashcards today.

LET'S PRACTICE

Write the meanings of these Latin sentences.

1. Amīcō nūntī amīcitiam populī nūntiātis.

   It means _You announce to the messenger's friend the people's friendliness._

2. Equus aquam prōvinciae amat, sed aquam silvae nōn amat.

   It means _The horse likes the province's water, but he does not like the forest's water._

3. Sociō puellae nūntiōs hodiē nārrāmus.

   It means _Today we tell the messages to the girl's comrade._

4. Memoriae dēlectant filiōs et filiās in īnsulā.

   It means _The memories please the sons and the daughters on the island._

5. Captīvum in vīllā gladiō servō.

   It means _I guard the captive in the farmhouse with a sword._

6. Laudās dīligentiam lēgātōrum in campō.

   It means _You praise the lieutenants' diligence on the plain._

7. Amīcō puellae carrōs fēminae nōn datis.

   It means _You do not give the woman's carts to the girl's friend._

8. Vocant filiī lēgātōs in campīs et in viīs.

   It means _The sons call the lieutenants on the plains and on the roads._

9. Cum audāciā socius in silvīs prōvinciae pugnat.

   It means _The comrade fights with boldness in the province's forests._

10. Exspectāmus poenam et fugam lēgātōrum rēgīnae.

    It means _We await the punishment and exile of the queen's envoys._

☐ I practiced my flashcards today.

136

Puellae carrum dō.　　It means **I give the cart** *to the girl.*
　　　　　　　　　　　　　　　　　　　　　or
　　　　　　　　　　　　　　I give the cart *for the girl.*

Now for more than one!

Puellīs* carrum dō.　　It means **I give the cart** *to the girls.*
　　　　　　　　　　　　　　　　　　　　　or
　　　　　　　　　　　　　　I give the cart *for the girls.*

Fīliō carrum dō.　　It means **I give the cart** *to the son.*
　　　　　　　　　　　　　　　　　　　　　or
　　　　　　　　　　　　　　I give the cart *for the son.*

Again . . . more than one!

Fīliīs* carrum dō.　　It means **I give the cart** *to the sons.*
　　　　　　　　　　　　　　　　　　　　　or
　　　　　　　　　　　　　　I give the cart *for the sons.*

Put a check in the box when you notice:

☑ This plural ending (īs) is the same for words like puella and words like fīlius.

*This ending (īs) is identical to the plural ending used to show the place ***where***. (See page 123.)

☐ I practiced my flashcards today. (Add the new cards.)

LET'S PRACTICE

Circle the correct Latin words.

1. (**Puellae,** Puellīs) carrum damus.

   It means **We give the cart to the girl.**

2. (Puellae, **Puellīs**) carrum damus.

   It means **We give the cart to the girls.**

---

3. Agricolae (equō, **equīs**) aquam portant.

   It means **The farmers carry water for the horses.**

4. Agricolae (**equō,** equīs) aquam portant.

   It means **The farmers carry water for the horse.**

---

5. (Lēgātō, **Lēgātīs**) rēginae gladiōs parātis.

   It means **You prepare the swords for the queen's envoys.**

6. (**Lēgātō,** Lēgātīs) rēginae gladiōs parātis.

   It means **You prepare the swords for the queen's envoy.**

---

7. Amīcus puellārum (**filiae,** filiīs) equum dat.

   It means **The friend of the girls gives the daughter a horse.**

8. Amīcus puellārum (filiae, **filiīs**) equum dat.

   It means **The friend of the girls gives the daughters a horse.**

☐ I practiced my flashcards today.

Latin Workbook - Level 3
Copyright © 1998 by Karen Mohs

LET'S PRACTICE

Choose the correct words for the sentences. Put them in the blanks. Then write what the sentences mean.

| audāciā - audācia |

1. Fīliōs cum **audāciā** superās.

It means You defeat the sons with boldness.

| Fīlius - Fīliō |

2. _____ **Fīliō** _____ tubās dant.

It means They give the trumpets to the son.

| īnsulae - īnsulā |

3. Portās nautam in _____ **īnsulā** .

It means You carry the sailor on the island.

| amīcitiā - amīcitiam |

4. Fīliās cum **amīcitiā** spectātis.

It means You look at the daughters with friendliness.

| nūntī - nūntiī |

5. In vīllā _____ **nūntī** _____ habitat.

It means He dwells in the messenger's villa.

| poēta - poētae |

6. Dō _____ **poētae** _____ epistulās.

It means I give the letters to the poet.

| Animīs - Animōs |

7. **Animōs** captīvōrum laudat.

It means He praises the spirits of the captives.

| ☐ I practiced my flashcards today. |

LET'S PRACTICE

Choose the best words for the sentences below. Then write what the sentences mean.

silvās	silvā	silva

1. In _____ **silvā** _____ equus servōs agricolae oppugnat.

   It means In the forest, the horse attacks the slaves of the farmer.

2. In īnsulā in aquā _____ **silva** _____ est.

   It means The forest is on the island in the water.

3. Populī _____ **silvās** _____ nātūrae hodiē nōn amant.

   It means Today the nations do not love the forests of nature.

appellat	appellātis	appellant

1. Agricola portās vīllae _____ **appellat** _____.

   It means The farmer names the gates of the farmhouse.

2. Nūntiī _____ **appellant** _____ agricolās in vīllīs.

   It means The messengers name the farmers in the farmhouses.

3. Vīllās agricolārum _____ **appellātis** _____.

   It means You name the farmhouses of the farmers.

☐ I practiced my flashcards today.

cūra

means

**care,
anxiety**

Write the Latin word that means **care**.

cūra

cūra

cūra

Write the Latin word that means **I stand**.

stō

stō

stō

stō

means

I stand

saepe

means

often

Write the Latin word that means **often**.

saepe

saepe

saepe

☐ I practiced my flashcards today. (Add the new cards.)

LET'S PRACTICE

Write the meanings of these Latin words.

poena	penalty, punishment	animus	mind, spirit
stāmus	we stand	socius	comrade, ally
fuga	flight, exile	vulnerō	I wound
exspectat	he awaits, he waits for	locus	place, location, situation
dīligentia	diligence, care	dēlectant	they please
servātis	you guard, you save, you keep	puer	boy
fābula	story	habitat	he lives, he dwells
nārrant	they relate, they tell	captīvus	captive
audācia	boldness, daring	nūntius	messenger, message, news
volō	I fly	temptāmus	we attempt
saepe	often	cūra	care, anxiety
carrus	cart, wagon	populus	people, nation, tribe
amicus	friend	ager	field, territory
superās	you surpass, you defeat	oppugnātis	you attack
cōpia	plenty, supply	crās	tomorrow

☐ I practiced my flashcards today.

Latin Workbook - Level 3
Copyright © 1998 by Karen Mohs

līberō

līberō means **I set free, I free**

Write the Latin word that means **I free**.

līberō

līberō

līberō

Write the Latin word that means **meanwhile**.

interim

interim

interim

interim

interim means **meanwhile**

cūr

cūr means **why** (a question)

Write the Latin word that means **why?**

cūr

cūr

cūr

☐ I practiced my flashcards today. (Add the new cards.)

LET'S PRACTICE

Choose the correct words for the sentences. Put them in the blanks.
Then write what the sentences mean.

cūr - stāmus

1. In aquā interim __stāmus__.

It means __Meanwhile, we stand in the water.__

īnsulā - īnsulās

2. Captivōs in __īnsulā__ līberās.

It means __You free the captives on the island.__

Gladiīs - Gladiī

3. __Gladiīs__ nōn saepe pugnō.

It means __I do not often fight with swords.__

poētārum - poētās

4. Cūr __poētās__ oppugnātis?

It means __Why do you attack the poets?__

puellīs - puellās

5. Quid __puellīs__ semper dat?

It means __What does he always give to the girls?__

viā - viae

6. Nūntium in __viā__ nūntiant.

It means __They announce the news on the road.__

carrus - carrōs

7. Servātis cum dīligentiā __carrōs__.

It means __You guard the carts with diligence.__

☐ I practiced my flashcards today.

144

dēmōnstrō

means

**I point out,
I show**

Write the Latin word that means **I show**.

dēmōnstrō

dēmōnstrō

dēmōnstrō

Write the Latin word that means **hour**.

hōra

hōra

hōra

hōra

means

hour

posteā

means

**after that time,
afterward, thereafter**

Write the Latin word that means **afterward**.

posteā

posteā

posteā

☐ I practiced my flashcards today. (Add the new cards.)

LET'S PRACTICE

Color the box pink if the English meaning matches the Latin word at the beginning of the row.

cōpia	supplies	supply	for the supplies
gladiī	of the sword	swords	sword
dēmōnstrāmus	we show	you show	they show
līberat	she frees	they free	I free
cūra	of anxiety	anxieties	anxiety
stās	it stands	you stand	we stand
posteā	thereafter	meanwhile	tomorrow
vītārum	of the life	of the lives	lives
volātis	you fly	he flies	they fly
hōrās	of the hour	hour	hours

☐ I practiced my flashcards today.

146

inopia

means

want, lack, need, poverty

Write the Latin word that means **want**.

inopia

inopia

inopia

Write the Latin word that means **wealth**.

pecūnia

pecūnia

pecūnia

pecūnia

means

wealth, money

cōnfīrmō

means

I strengthen, I encourage, I declare

Write the Latin word that means **I declare**.

cōnfīrmō

cōnfīrmō

cōnfīrmō

☐ I practiced my flashcards today. (Add the new cards.)

LET'S PRACTICE

Write the Latin words.

yesterday	herī
what?	quid
with	cum
we fly	volāmus
tomorrow	crās
I fight	pugnō
she tells	nārrat
but	sed
we grant	damus
afterward	posteā
of the streets	viārum
they praise	laudant

it likes	amat
I defeat	superō
where?	ubi
we stand	stāmus
I report	nūntiō
they call	vocant
of the sons	fīliōrum
I keep	servō
already	iam
why?	cūr
long	diū
he carries	portat

☐ I practiced my flashcards today.

148

tum

tum means **then, at that time**

Write the Latin word that means **then**.

tum

tum

tum

Write the Latin word that means **I shout**.

clāmō

clāmō

clāmō

clāmō

clāmō means **I shout**

dominus

dominus means **master, Lord, owner**

Write the Latin word that means **master**.

dominus

dominus

dominus

☐ I practiced my flashcards today. (Add the new cards.)

LET'S PRACTICE

Match the words to their meanings.

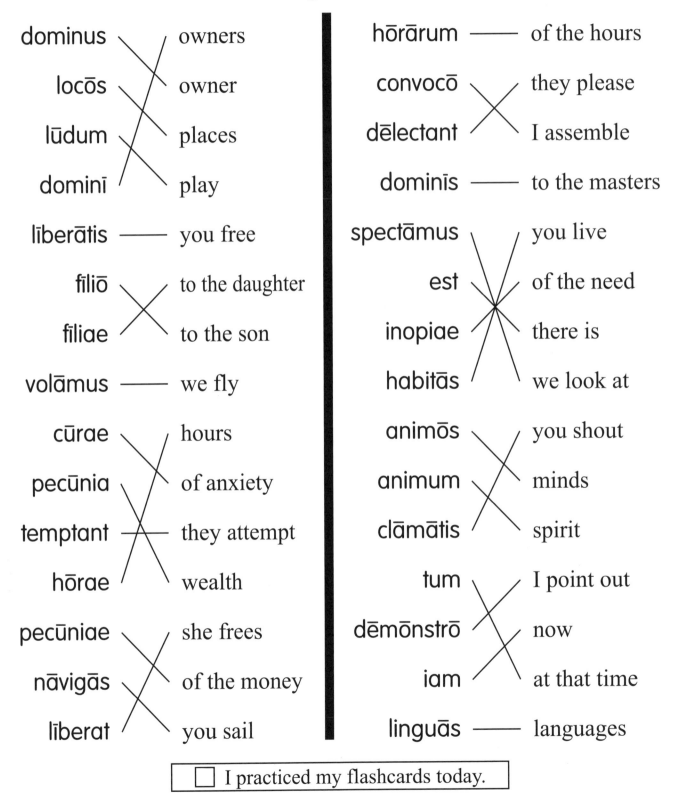

dominus	owners
locōs	owner
lūdum	places
dominī	play

liberātis ——	you free
filiō	to the daughter
filiae	to the son
volāmus ——	we fly

cūrae	hours
pecūnia	of anxiety
temptant	they attempt
hōrae	wealth

pecūniae	she frees
nāvigās	of the money
līberat	you sail

hōrārum ——	of the hours
convocō	they please
dēlectant	I assemble
dominīs ——	to the masters

spectāmus	you live
est	of the need
inopiae	there is
habitās	we look at

animōs	you shout
animum	minds
clāmātis	spirit

tum	I point out
dēmōnstrō	now
iam	at that time
linguās ——	languages

☐ I practiced my flashcards today.

ambulō

ambulō means **I stroll, I walk**

Write the Latin word that means **I walk**.

ambulō

ambulō

ambulō

Write the Latin word that means **badly**.

male

male

male

male

male means **badly, insufficiently**

---

numerus

numerus means **number, group**

Write the Latin word that means **number**.

numerus

numerus

numerus

☐ I practiced my flashcards today. (Add the new cards.)

LET'S PRACTICE

Color the box brown if the Latin word matches the English meaning at the beginning of the row.

they show	dēmōnstrat	dēmōnstrō	dēmōnstrant
badly	cūr	tum	male
I shout	clāmāmus	clāmō	clāmās
we set free	liberāmus	liberātis	liberant
master	dominī	dominus	dominōs
he stands	stāmus	stant	stat
poverty	inopia	inopiae	inopiās
you stroll	ambulāmus	ambulātis	ambulō
money	pecūniae	pecūnia	pecūniās
you declare	cōnfīrmant	cōnfīrmāmus	cōnfīrmās

☐ I practiced my flashcards today.

152

LET'S PRACTICE

Write the Latin words.

reason	causa	she labors	labōrat
hour	hōra	meanwhile	interim
often	saepe	they are	sunt
we shout	clāmāmus	then	tum
badly	male	I declare	cōnfīrmō
he attempts	temptat	tomorrow	crās
thereafter	posteā	he summons	convocat
we free	līberāmus	we like	amāmus
he reports	nūntiat	group	numerus
I walk	ambulō	why?	cūr
penalty	poena	we fly	volāmus
they keep	servant	anxiety	cūra

☐ I practiced my flashcards today.

LET'S PRACTICE

Match the words to their meanings.

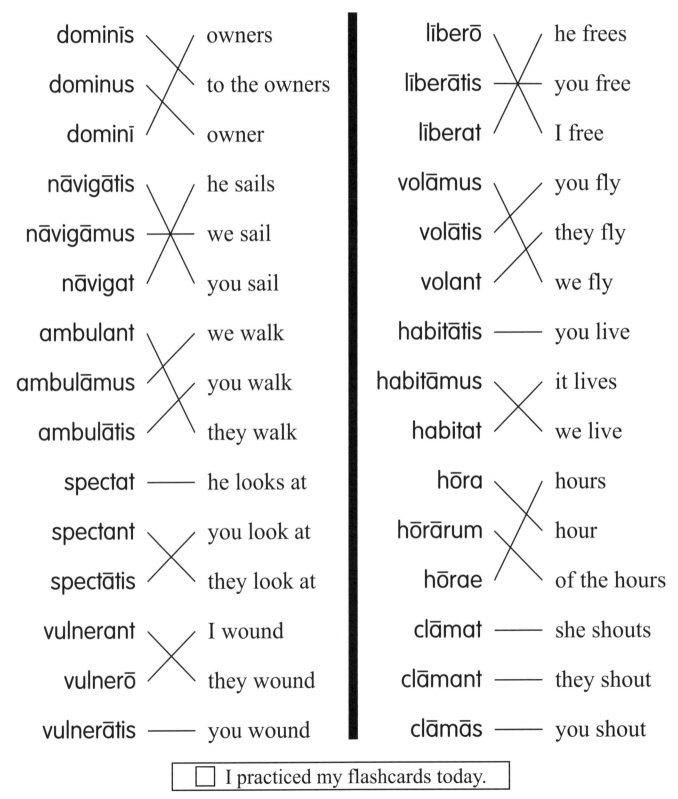

dominīs	owners
dominus	to the owners
dominī	owner
nāvigātis	he sails
nāvigāmus	we sail
nāvigat	you sail
ambulant	we walk
ambulāmus	you walk
ambulātis	they walk
spectat	he looks at
spectant	you look at
spectātis	they look at
vulnerant	I wound
vulnerō	they wound
vulnerātis	you wound

līberō	he frees
līberātis	you free
līberat	I free
volāmus	you fly
volātis	they fly
volant	we fly
habitātis	you live
habitāmus	it lives
habitat	we live
hōra	hours
hōrārum	hour
hōrae	of the hours
clāmat	she shouts
clāmant	they shout
clāmās	you shout

☐ I practiced my flashcards today.

154

LET'S PRACTICE

Color the box orange if the English meaning matches the Latin word at the beginning of the row.

numerī	of the group	group	for the group
locī	of the places	place	places
inopia	poverty	of poverty	for poverty
dominōrum	of the lords	for the lords	lords
captīvō	captive	of the captive	to the captive
rēgīnae	queen	for the queen	of the queens
puellīs	girl	to the girl	to the girls
male	insufficiently	for a long time	along with
pecūniam	wealth	of wealth	for wealth
hōrās	of hours	hour	hours

☐ I practiced my flashcards today.

LET'S PRACTICE

Color the popsicle purple if the words inside mean the same.

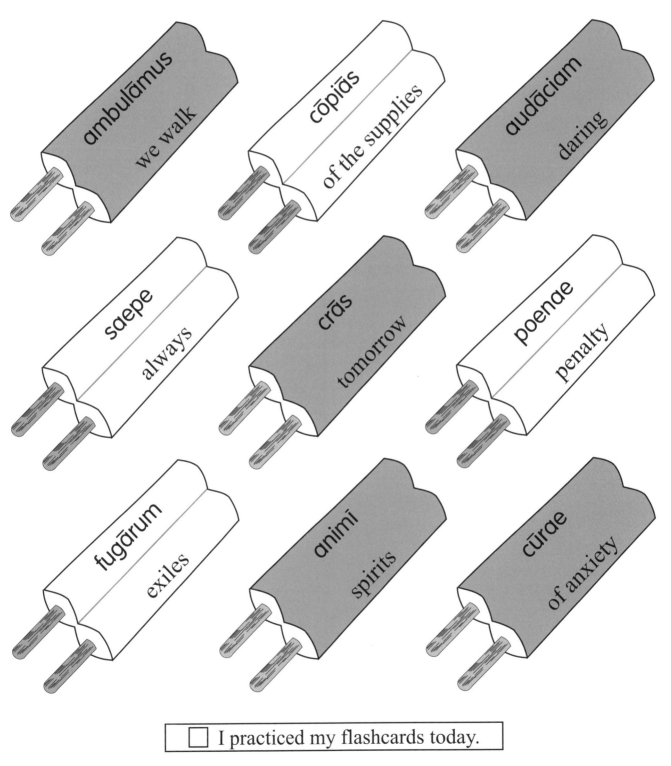

ambulāmus — we walk

cōpiās — of the supplies

audāciam — daring

saepe — always

crās — tomorrow

poenae — penalty

fugārum — exiles

animī — spirits

cūrae — of anxiety

☐ I practiced my flashcards today.

LET'S PRACTICE

Put checks in the boxes of the correct Latin sentences.

You always shout the news of the hour to the captives in the cart.
☑ Captivīs in carrō nūntium hōrae semper clāmātis. ☐ Captivō in carrīs nūntium hōrae semper clāmātis. ☐ Captivīs in carrō nūntium hōrae semper clāmāmus.
The poet walks on the road and prepares for the game with care.
☐ Poētae in viā ambulant et lūdum cum dīligentiā parant. ☑ Poēta in viā ambulat et lūdum cum dīligentiā parat. ☐ Poēta in viīs ambulat et lūdās cum dīligentiā parat.
We stand on the plain and look at the farmer's horses and villas.
☐ In campīs stāt et equōs et vīllās agricolae spectāt. ☐ In campō stāmus et equus et vīlla agricolae spectāmus. ☑ In campō stāmus et equōs et vīllās agricolae spectāmus.
The daughters please the women, but the sons point out the reasons.
☐ Fīlia fēminās dēlectat, sed filiī causās dēmōnstrant. ☐ Fīliī fēminās dēlectant, sed filiae causās dēmōnstrant. ☑ Fīliae fēminās dēlectant, sed filiī causās dēmōnstrant.
Why do the friends on the island attack the sailors in the forest with swords?
☑ Cūr amīcī in īnsulā nautās in silvā gladiīs oppugnant? ☐ Ubi amīcī in īnsulā nautās in silvā gladiīs oppugnant? ☐ Cum amīcī in īnsulā nautās in silvā gladiīs oppugnant?

☐ I practiced my flashcards today.

LET'S PRACTICE

Put the endings in the boxes on the Latin words in the sentences.

ārum ō	1. Cōnfirmō numerōs fēminārum.
ōrum ōs	It means **I encourage the groups of women.**

ātis ōs	2. Captīvōs cum audāciā nunc līberāmus.
āmus ā	It means **We now free the captives with boldness.**

ās ōs	3. Poētae portās et viās dēmōnstrās.
ās ae	It means **You show the poet the gates and streets.**

ās us	4. Ubi fīlius lēgātum vulnerat?
at um	It means **Where does the son wound the envoy?**

at ae	5. Quid nautae agricola dat?
a ā	It means **What does the farmer give to the sailor?**

ae at	6. Linguam patriae laudat.
ant am	It means **She praises the language of the native land.**

☐ I practiced my flashcards today.

LET'S PRACTICE

Fill in the blanks with the correct words from the boxes on the right.
Then write the meanings of the sentences.

1. Occupāmus __caṗtīvum__ gladiō.

   It means _We seize the captive with a sword._

   | captīvus |
   | captīvum |
   | captīvōrum |

2. Puella in terrā rēgīnae __habitat__.

   It means _The girl dwells in the queen's land._

   | habitat |
   | habitō |
   | habitant |

3. Cum amīcitiā fābulam __nārrant__.

   It means _They tell the story with friendliness._

   | nautās |
   | nārrant |
   | nūntiārum |

4. __Amīcīs__ fīlī tubās dō.

   It means _I give trumpets to the friends of the son._

   | Amīcīs |
   | Amīcus |
   | Amīcās |

5. Lūdōs puellārum in __villā__ laudās.

   It means _You praise the girls' games in the villa._

   | villā |
   | villa |
   | villae |

6. Cūr __populōs__ hodiē convocātis?

   It means _Why do you summon the nations today?_

   | populus |
   | populōrum |
   | populōs |

7. Lēgātus gladiōs in equō __portat__.

   It means _The envoy carries the swords on the horse._

   | portāmus |
   | portat |
   | portant |

☐ I practiced my flashcards today.

LET'S PRACTICE

Choose the best words for the sentences below. Then write what the sentences mean.

spectat	spectant	spectās

1. Inopiam numerōrum servōrum in prōvinciā **spectās**.

   It means _You look at the poverty of the groups of slaves in the province._

2. Cūr fēmina **spectat** terram agricolārum?

   It means _Why does the woman look at the land of the farmers?_

3. Nautae semper **spectant** aquās īnsulārum.

   It means _The sailors always look at the waters of the islands._

fīliīs	fīlia	fīliae

1. Dominīs **fīlia** fābulās carrōrum nārrat.

   It means _The daughter tells the stories of the carts to the owners._

2. Das **fīliīs** poētārum tubam.

   It means _You give the trumpet to the daughters (or sons) of the poets._

3. Interim **fīliae** captīvōrum in viīs stant.

   It means _Meanwhile, the daughters of the captives stand in the roads._

☐ I practiced my flashcards today.

160

FINAL REVIEW

Match the words to their meanings.

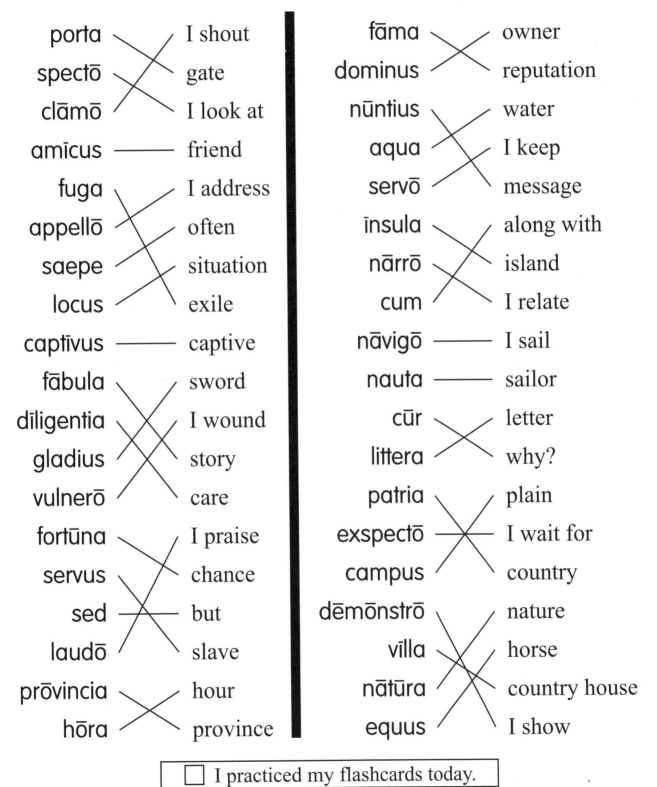

porta	I shout
spectō	gate
clāmō	I look at
amīcus	friend
fuga	I address
appellō	often
saepe	situation
locus	exile
captīvus	captive
fābula	sword
dīligentia	I wound
gladius	story
vulnerō	care
fortūna	I praise
servus	chance
sed	but
laudō	slave
prōvincia	hour
hōra	province

fāma	owner
dominus	reputation
nūntius	water
aqua	I keep
servō	message
īnsula	along with
nārrō	island
cum	I relate
nāvigō	I sail
nauta	sailor
cūr	letter
littera	why?
patria	plain
exspectō	I wait for
campus	country
dēmōnstrō	nature
vīlla	horse
nātūra	country house
equus	I show

☐ I practiced my flashcards today.

FINAL REVIEW

Match the words to their meanings.

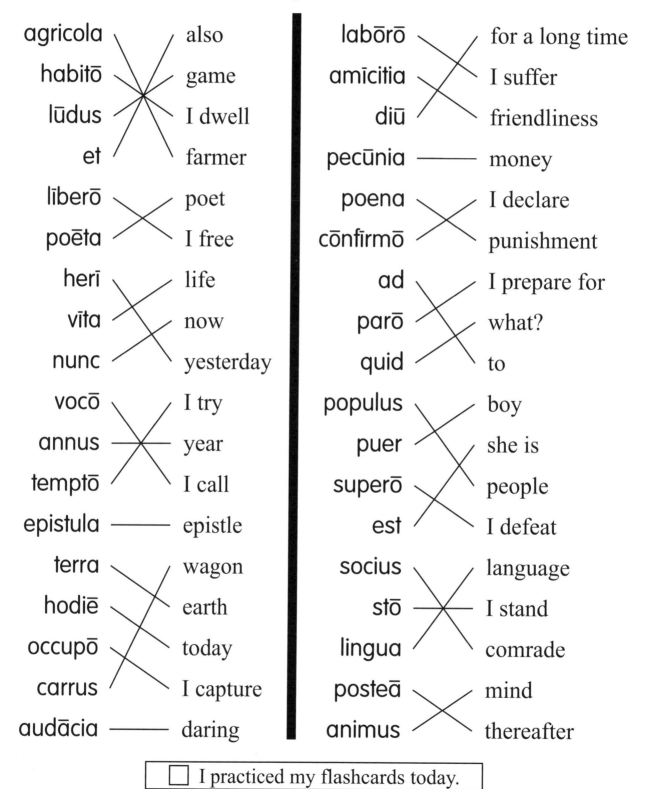

agricola	also
habitō	game
lūdus	I dwell
et	farmer
līberō	poet
poēta	I free
herī	life
vīta	now
nunc	yesterday
vocō	I try
annus	year
temptō	I call
epistula	epistle
terra	wagon
hodiē	earth
occupō	today
carrus	I capture
audācia	daring

labōrō	for a long time
amīcitia	I suffer
diū	friendliness
pecūnia	money
poena	I declare
cōnfirmō	punishment
ad	I prepare for
parō	what?
quid	to
populus	boy
puer	she is
superō	people
est	I defeat
socius	language
stō	I stand
lingua	comrade
posteā	mind
animus	thereafter

☐ I practiced my flashcards today.

162

FINAL REVIEW

Match the words to their meanings.

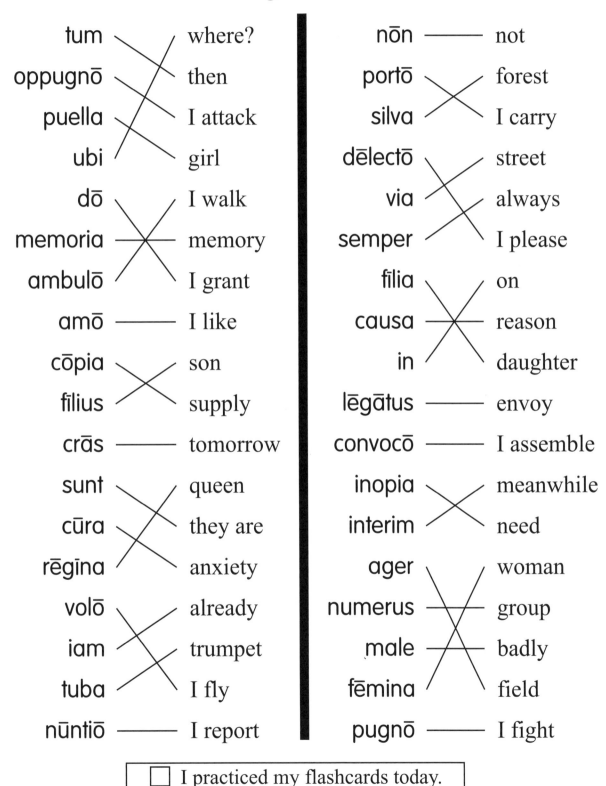

Latin	Meaning
tum	where?
oppugnō	then
puella	I attack
ubi	girl
dō	I walk
memoria	memory
ambulō	I grant
amō	I like
cōpia	son
filius	supply
crās	tomorrow
sunt	queen
cūra	they are
rēgīna	anxiety
volō	already
iam	trumpet
tuba	I fly
nūntiō	I report

Latin	Meaning
nōn	not
portō	forest
silva	I carry
dēlectō	street
via	always
semper	I please
filia	on
causa	reason
in	daughter
lēgātus	envoy
convocō	I assemble
inopia	meanwhile
interim	need
ager	woman
numerus	group
male	badly
fēmina	field
pugnō	I fight

☐ I practiced my flashcards today.

FINAL REVIEW

Draw pictures for these sentences.

Poētae in patriā saepe ambulant, et fīliōs fēminārum laudant.

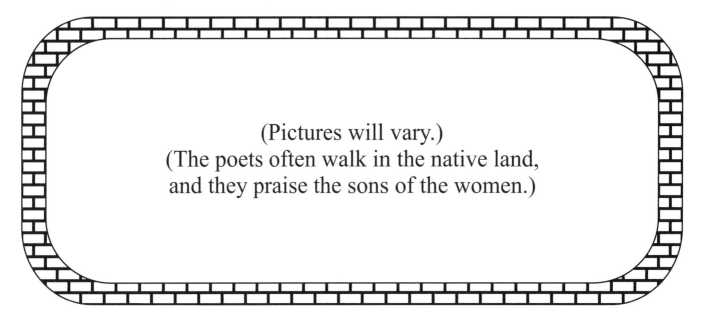

(Pictures will vary.)
(The poets often walk in the native land,
and they praise the sons of the women.)

Cum audāciā nūntium clāmāmus, sed poenam nōn amāmus.

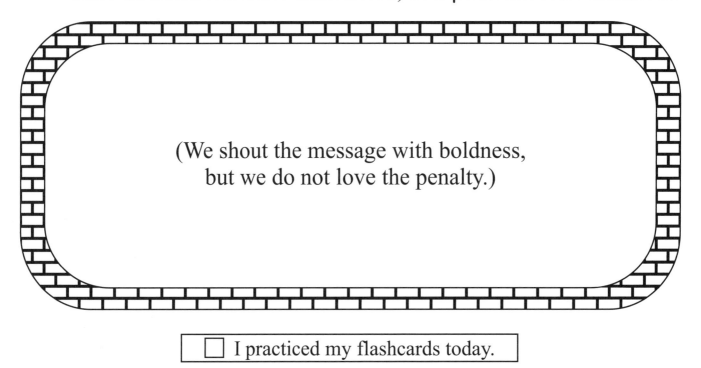

(We shout the message with boldness,
but we do not love the penalty.)

☐ I practiced my flashcards today.

FINAL REVIEW

Match the correct Latin sentences to their meanings below.

    a. Cūr in īnsulīs diū habitō?

    b. Quid fēminae in aquā tum exspectant?

    c. Cūr in carrīs servōs semper līberātis?

    d. Ubi volātis et ubi ambulātis?

    e. Cūr amīcus iam oppugnat prōvinciam?

    f. Quid fīliīs sociōrum datis?

    g. Ubi lēgātī inopiās populōrum cōnfirmant?

    h. Cūr rēgīnae poētās in silvīs servant?

(f) 1. What do you give to the sons of the comrades?

(d) 2. Where do you fly, and where do you walk?

(h) 3. Why do the queens keep the poets in the forests?

(b) 4. What do the women in the water wait for at that time?

(a) 5. Why do I dwell on the islands for a long time?

(e) 6. Why does the friend attack the province already?

(g) 7. Where do the envoys declare the needs of the nations?

(c) 8. Why do you always free the slaves in the wagons?

    ☐ I practiced my flashcards today.

FINAL REVIEW

Write the meanings of these Latin words.

dēlectō	I please	dēlectāmus	we please
dēlectās	you (sing.) please	dēlectātis	you (pl.) please
dēlectat	he (she, it) pleases	dēlectant	they please

vīlla	the farmhouse	vīllae	the farmhouses
vīllae	of the farmhouse	vīllārum	of the farmhouses
vīllae	to (or for) the farmhouse	vīllīs	to (or for) the farmhouses
vīllam	the farmhouse	vīllās	the farmhouses
in vīllā	in the farmhouse	in vīllīs	in the farmhouses

clāmō	I shout	clāmāmus	we shout
clāmās	you (sing.) shout	clāmātis	you (pl.) shout
clāmat	he (she, it) shouts	clāmant	they shout

locus	the place	locī	the places
locī	of the place	locōrum	of the places
locō	to (or for) the place	locīs	to (or for) the places
locum	the place	locōs	the places
in locō	in the place	in locīs	in the places

☐ I practiced my flashcards today.

Latin Workbook - Level 3
Copyright © 1998 by Karen Mohs

FINAL REVIEW

Write the sentences using the words on the right.

1. **In equō stāmus.**
   It means **We stand on the horse.**

2. **Equī in aquā stant.**
   It means **The horses stand in the water.**

3. **Stās et portās aquam.**
   It means **You stand and carry the water.**

aquā
aquam
equī
equō
et
in
in
portās
stāmus
stant
stās

4. **Fīliō clāmō.**
   It means **I shout to the son.**

5. **Fīliī amīcīs clāmant.**
   It means **The sons shout to the friends.**

6. **Amīcus fīliī clāmat.**
   It means **The friend of the son shouts.**

amīcīs
amīcus
clāmant
clāmat
clāmō
fīliī
fīliī
fīliō

☐ I practiced my flashcards today.

FINAL REVIEW

Color the butterfly if the words on its wings mean the same.

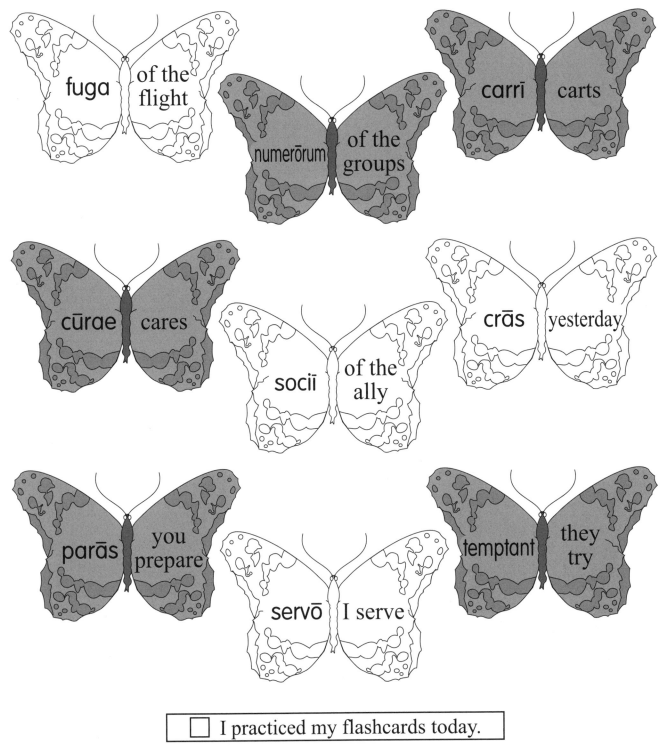

☐ I practiced my flashcards today.

FINAL REVIEW

Write the meanings of these Latin sentences.

1. Cūr lēgātōs gladiīs oppugnāmus?

   It means _Why do we attack the lieutenants with the swords?_

2. Hōram poenae diū exspectātis.

   It means _You await the hour of punishment for a long time._

3. Fēminīs nautārum epistulās nunc damus.

   It means _We now give the letters to the sailors' wives._

4. Dominō prōvinciās in terrā hodiē dēmōnstrō.

   It means _Today I show the master the provinces in the country._

5. Captīvus in carrō stat, et populō clāmat.

   It means _The captive stands in the wagon, and he shouts to the people._

6. Numerī fīliārum semper cōnfirmant in īnsulā agricolās.

   It means _Groups of daughters always encourage the farmers on the island._

7. Portam in equō cum dīligentiā interim portātis.

   It means _Meanwhile, you carry the gate on the horse with care._

8. Cūr agricolae in campīs rēginīs terrae labōrant?

   It means _Why do the farmers labor in the fields for the queens of the land?_

9. Ubi fīlius poētae servat pecūniam et aquam?

   It means _Where does the son of the poet keep the money and the water?_

10. Posteā lēgātī male pugnant, et rēginam nōn amant.

    It means _Thereafter, the envoys fight badly, and they do not love the queen._

☐ I practiced my flashcards today.

PUZZLE TIME

Think of the meanings of the English words. Then write the Latin words on the puzzle below.

across		down	
3.	on	1.	I attack
7.	wealth	2.	why?
8.	I dwell	3.	already
9.	I love	4.	language
10.	I stand	5.	I give
12.	where?	6.	friendship
15.	now	8.	hour
16.	boldness	11.	flight
18.	reason	13.	poverty
19.	penalty	14.	insufficiently
22.	I walk	17.	anxiety
23.	reputation	20.	to
24.	often	21.	then

Crossword grid answers:

- 3 across: in
- 7 across: pecūnia
- 8 across: habitō
- 9 across: amō
- 10 across: stō
- 12 across: ubi
- 15 across: nunc
- 16 across: audācia
- 18 across: causa
- 19 across: poena
- 22 across: ambulō
- 23 across: fāma
- 24 across: saepe

- 1 down: oppugnō
- 2 down: cūr
- 3 down: iam
- 4 down: lingua
- 5 down: dō
- 6 down: amīcitia
- 8 down: hōra
- 11 down: fī
- 13 down: inopia
- 14 down: male
- 17 down: cūra
- 20 down: ad
- 21 down: tum

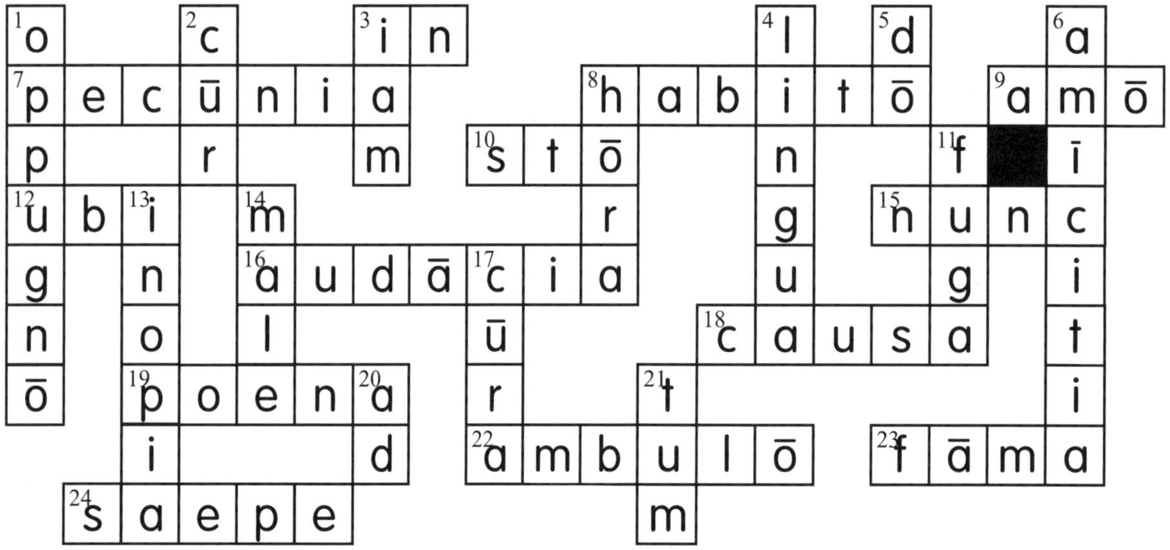

☐ I practiced my flashcards today.

170

Latin - English Glossary

a

ad - to, near, toward, for, at (14)

ager - field, territory (17)

agricola - farmer (12)

ambulō - I stroll, I walk (151)

amīcitia - friendship, friendliness (22)

amīcus - friend (17)

amō - I love, I like (22)

animus - mind, spirit (105)

annus - year (23)

appellō - I address, I call, I name (43)

aqua - water (12)

audācia - boldness, daring (103)

c

campus - field, plain (19)

captivus - captive (101)

carrus - cart, wagon (105)

causa - cause, reason (53)

clāmō - I shout (149)

cōnfirmō - I strengthen, I encourage, I declare (147)

convocō - I call together, I assemble, I summon (55)

cōpia - plenty, supply (93)

crās - tomorrow (105)

cum - along with, with (20)

cūr - why? (143)

cūra - care, anxiety (141)

d

dēlectō - I please (53)

dēmōnstrō - I point out, I show (145)

dīligentia - diligence, care (55)

diū - for a long time, long (95)

d

dō - I give, I grant (11)

dominus - master, Lord, owner (149)

e

epistula - letter, epistle (49)

equus - horse (22)

est - he is, she is, it is, there is (12)

et - and, also, even (13)

exspectō - I await, I wait for (49)

f

fābula - story (51)

fāma - report, rumor, reputation (47)

fēmina - woman, wife (12)

filia - daughter (21)

filius - son (21)

fortūna - fortune, chance, luck (16)

fuga - flight, exile (97)

g

gladius - sword (24)

h

habitō - I live, I dwell (51)

herī - yesterday (99)

hodiē - today (103)

hōra - hour (145)

i

iam - now, already (97)

in - into, against, in, on (93)

inopia - want, lack, need, poverty (147)

īnsula - island (13)

interim - meanwhile (143)

l

labōrō - I labor, I suffer, I am hard pressed (53)

laudō - I praise (14)

lēgātus - lieutenant, envoy (43)

līberō - I set free, I free (143)

lingua - tongue, language (22)

littera - letter (of the alphabet); (if plural: epistle, letter) (20)

locus - place, location, situation (101)

lūdus - game, play, school (43)

m

male - badly, insufficiently (151)

memoria - memory (15)

n

nārrō - I relate, I tell (47)

nātūra - nature (19)

nauta - sailor (20)

nāvigō - I sail (15)

nōn - not (14)

numerus - number, group (151)

nunc - now (51)

nūntiō - I announce, I report (45)

nūntius - messenger, message, news (45)

o

occupō - I seize, I capture (19)

oppugnō - I attack (95)

p

parō - I prepare, I prepare for (17)

patria - country, native land (21)

pecūnia - wealth, money (147)

poena - penalty, punishment (99)

Note: The number in parentheses indicates the page on which the vocabulary word is introduced.

APPENDIX

Latin - English Glossary

poēta - poet (23)
populus - people, nation, tribe (47)
porta - gate (15)
portō - I carry (16)
posteā - after that time, afterward,
    thereafter (145)
prōvincia - province (24)
puella - girl (11)
puer - boy (11)
pugnō - I fight (23)

q
quid - what? (16)

r
rēgīna - queen (49)

s
saepe - often (141)
sed - but (15)
semper - always (101)
servō - I guard, I save, I keep (99)
servus - slave (45)
silva - forest (13)
socius - comrade, ally (55)
spectō - I look at (19)
stō - I stand (141)
sunt - they are, there are (13)
superō - I surpass, I defeat (93)

t
temptō - I try, I attempt (97)
terra - earth, land, country (23)
tuba - trumpet (17)
tum - then, at that time (149)

u
ubi - where? (21)

v
via - road, way, street (16)
vīlla - farmhouse, country house,
    villa (20)
vīta - life (14)
vocō - I call (11)
volō - I fly (103)
vulnerō - I wound (95)

APPENDIX

English - Latin Glossary

a

address - appellō
after that time - posteā
afterward - posteā
against - in
ally - socius
along with - cum
already - iam
also - et
always - semper
and - et
announce - nūntiō
anxiety - cūra
are - sunt
assemble - convocō
at - ad
at that time - tum
attack - oppugnō
attempt - temptō
await - exspectō

b

badly - male
boldness - audācia
boy - puer
but - sed

c

call - vocō, appellō
call together - convocō
captive - captīvus
capture - occupō
care - dīligentia, cūra
carry - portō
cart - carrus
cause - causa
chance - fortūna
comrade - socius
country - patria, terra

country house - vīlla

d

daring - audācia
daughter - fīlia
declare - cōnfirmō
defeat - superō
diligence - dīligentia
dwell - habitō

e

earth - terra
encourage - cōnfirmō
envoy - lēgātus
epistle - littera (plural), epistula
even - et
exile - fuga

f

farmer - agricola
farmhouse - vīlla
field - ager, campus
fight - pugnō
flight - fuga
fly - volō
for - ad
for a long time - diū
forest - silva
fortune - fortūna
free - līberō
friend - amīcus
friendliness - amīcitia
friendship - amīcitia

g

game - lūdus
gate - porta
girl - puella
give - dō

grant - dō
group - numerus
guard - servō

h

hard pressed - labōrō
horse - equus
hour - hōra

i

in - in
insufficiently - male
into - in
is - est
island - īnsula

k

keep - servō

l

labor - labōrō
lack - inopia
land - terra
language - lingua
letter - littera, epistula
lieutenant - lēgātus
life - vīta
like - amō
live - habitō
location - locus
long - diū
look at - spectō
Lord - dominus
love - amō
luck - fortūna

m

master - dominus
meanwhile - interim

APPENDIX

English - Latin Glossary

memory - memoria
message - nūntius
messenger - nūntius
mind - animus
money - pecūnia

n
name - appellō
nation - populus
native land - patria
nature - nātūra
near - ad
need - inopia
news - nūntius
not - nōn
now - nunc, iam
number - numerus

o
often - saepe
on - in
owner - dominus

p
penalty - poena
people - populus
place - locus
plain - campus
play - lūdus
please - dēlectō
plenty - cōpia
poet - poēta
point out - dēmōnstrō
poverty - inopia
praise - laudō
prepare - parō
prepare for - parō
province - prōvincia
punishment - poena

q
queen - rēgina

r
reason - causa
relate - nārrō
report - nūntiō, fāma
reputation - fāma
road - via
rumor - fāma

s
sail - nāvigō
sailor - nauta
save - servō
school - lūdus
seize - occupō
set free - liberō
shout - clāmō
show - dēmōnstrō
situation - locus
slave - servus
son - filius
spirit - animus
stand - stō
story - fābula
street - via
strengthen - cōnfirmō
stroll - ambulō
suffer - labōrō
summon - convocō
supply - cōpia
surpass - superō
sword - gladius

t
tell - nārrō
territory - ager
then - tum

thereafter - posteā
to - ad
today - hodiē
tomorrow - crās
tongue - lingua
toward - ad
tribe - populus
trumpet - tuba
try - temptō

v
villa - vīlla

w
wagon - carrus
wait for - exspectō
walk - ambulō
want - inopia
water - aqua
way - via
wealth - pecūnia
what? - quid
where? - ubi
why? - cūr
wife - fēmina
with - cum
woman - fēmina
wound - vulnerō

y
year - annus
yesterday - herī

APPENDIX

Latin Alphabet

Capital Letter	Small Letter	Pronunciation		Capital Letter	Small Letter	Pronunciation
Ā	ā	a in *father*		N	n	n in *nut*
A	a	a in *idea*		Ō**	ō**	o in *note*
B	b	b in *boy*		O**	o**	o in *omit*
C	c	c in *cat*		P	p	p in *pit*
D	d	d in *dog*		Q	q	qu in *quit*
Ē	ē	ey in *obey*		R	r	r in *run*
E	e	e in *bet*		S	s	s in *sit*
F	f	f in *fan*		T	t	t in *tag*
G	g	g in *go*		Ū	ū	u in *rule*
H	h	h in *hat*		U	u	u in *put*
Ī	ī	i in *machine*		V	v	w in *way*
I*	i*	i in *sit*		X	x	ks in *socks*
K	k	k in *king*		Ȳ	ȳ	form lips to say "**oo**" but say "**ee**" instead (held longer)
L	l	l in *land*		Y	y	form lips to say "**oo**" but say "**ee**" instead (held shorter)
M	m	m in *man*		Z	z	dz in *adze*

*When functioning as a consonant, i has the sound of **y** in *youth*. (See **Special Consonants** below.)
**The ō and the o both have a long o sound, but the ō is held longer.

Special Sounds

Diphthongs

Letters	Pronunciation
ae	*aye*
au	ow in *now*
ei	ei in *neighbor*
eu	*ay-oo*
oe	oy in *joy*
ui	uee in *queen*

Special Consonants

Letters	Pronunciation
bs	*ps*
bt	*pt*
ch	ch in *character*
gu	gu in *anguish*
i	y in *youth*
ph	ph in *phone*
su	su in *suave*
th	th in *thick*

APPENDIX

Word Order

Word order in Latin is not the same as word order in English. In Latin, since the ending determines the role the word plays in the sentence, word order is generally used for emphasis. However, there is a tendency to put the verb last.

Moods of the Latin Verb

Latin verbs are classified according to mood.

The **indicative** *mood* is used to make an assertion or to ask a question.
The **subjunctive** *mood* is used to describe an action that is not real.
The **imperative** *mood* is used to make a command.

A **participle** is a verbal adjective, and an **infinitive** is a verbal noun.

Voices of the Latin Verb

Voices of the Latin verb:

Active Voice: The subject of the sentence is ***doing an action***.
    Example: The man loves the woman.

Passive Voice: The subject of the sentence is *receiving an action*.
    Example: The man is being loved by the woman.

Gender and Case of the Latin Noun

The three genders of Latin nouns are masculine, feminine, and neuter.

Latin nouns are declined using five main *cases*.

The subject of the sentence as well as a noun "linked" to the subject with a linking verb (e.g. *is* or *are*) belong in the **nominative** case. Possession is expressed with the **genitive** case. The indirect object belongs in the **dative** case. The direct object belongs in the **accusative** case. The **ablative** case is used to express special relationships. These cases have other important uses as well.

APPENDIX

First Conjugation

A Latin verb belongs to the first conjugation if its second principal part ends in -āre. Its present tense stem can be found by dropping the -re of the second principal part. (Principal parts will be taught later in this series.) The **present tense** is used to describe actions happening in the present time.

Present Active Indicative
(present indicative verb stem + personal ending)

	Singular	Meaning	Plural	Meaning
1st Person	amō	I like (*or* I am liking) (*or* I do like)	amāmus	we like (*or* we are liking) (*or* we do like)
2nd Person	amās	you (s.) like (*or* you are liking) (*or* you do like)	amātis	you (pl.) like (*or* you are liking) (*or* you do like)
3rd Person	amat	he (she, it) likes (*or* he is liking) (*or* he does like)	amant	they like (*or* they are liking) (*or* they do like)

First Declension

A Latin noun belongs to the first declension if the genitive singular ends in -ae. Remove the -ae from the genitive singular to find the stem. These nouns are usually feminine, unless they describe males in Latin culture such as sailors, poets, or farmers.

	Singular	Meaning	Plural	Meaning
Nominative	puella	a girl (*or* the girl)	puellae	girls (*or* the girls)
Genitive	puellae	of a girl (*or* of the girl)	puellārum	of girls (*or* of the girls)
Dative	puellae	to/for a girl (*or* to/for the girl)	puellīs	to/for girls (*or* to/for the girls)
Accusative	puellam	a girl (*or* the girl)	puellās	girls (*or* the girls)
Abative	puellā	by/with* a girl (*or* by/with* the girl)	puellīs	by/with* girls (*or* by/with* the girls)

*The translations given above are just a sampling of the many possible meanings of the ablative case.

APPENDIX

Second Declension

A Latin noun belongs to the second declension if the genitive singular ends in -ī. Remove the -ī from the genitive singular to find the stem. If a second declension nominative ends in -us, it is usually masculine.

	Singular	Meaning	Plural	Meaning
Nominative	amīcus	a friend (*or* the friend)	amīcī	friends (*or* the friends)
Genitive	amīcī	of a friend (*or* of the friend)	amīcōrum	of friends (*or* of the friends)
Dative	amīcō	to/for a friend (*or* to/for the friend)	amīcīs	to/for friends (*or* to/for the friends)
Accusative	amīcum	a friend (*or* the friend)	amīcōs	friends (*or* the friends)
Abative	amīcō	by/with* a friend (*or* by/with* the friend)	amīcīs	by/with* friends (*or* by/with* the friends)

*The translations given above are just a sampling of the many possible meanings of the ablative case.

Second Declension -ius

A Latin second declension -ius noun is declined like a second declension -us noun except in the genitive singular. The expected genitive singular -iī of these -ius nouns is shortened to -ī. However, the stem retains the -i- [soci-].

	Singular	Meaning	Plural	Meaning
Nominative	socius	an ally (*or* the ally)	sociī	allies (*or* the allies)
Genitive	socī	of an ally (*or* of the ally)	sociōrum	of allies (*or* of the allies)
Dative	sociō	to/for an ally (*or* to/for the ally)	sociīs	to/for allies (*or* to/for the allies)
Accusative	socium	an ally (*or* the ally)	sociōs	allies (*or* the allies)
Abative	sociō	by/with* an ally (*or* by/with* the ally)	sociīs	by/with* allies (*or* by/with* the allies)

*The translations given above are just a sampling of the many possible meanings of the ablative case.

APPENDIX

Index

APPENDIX

Flashcard Tips

1. Remember to practice flashcards daily.

2. Do not move ahead in the workbook if your student is struggling for mastery. Review the flashcards every day until your student is confident and ready to learn more.

3. For each noun and verb ending, there are some "example" words to help your student become familiar with the endings. Please help your student apply these endings to all vocabulary words.

4. When the number of cards becomes too cumbersome to do in one day, remove the cards your student knows without hesitation and put them in an "Occasional Practice" stack. Review the "Occasional Practice" stack once a week.